AGON Institute of Sports Ministry Series, vol. 4

D1733355

The Saving of Sports Ministry: The Soteriology of Sports Outreach

Dr. Greg Linville

OVERWHELMING

PRESS

This book is dedicated to Norah, my awesome granddaughter!
You bring joy to my heart and a smile to my face every time we're together.
Here's hoping and praying that you will embrace Jesus
as your personal Lord and Savior and thus we will be able to extend
our joyous times together for all of eternity.

Table of Contents

ENDORSEMENTS

"Greg's latest book is an important read! I fully believe in and am passionate about the mission of sports in the local church. We all have an obligation to carry on this mission and this book offers some practical principles to help us advance the Gospel of Jesus Christ through sports."

— Neal Gossett
Campus Pastor, South East Christian Church
Former Sports Outreach Director & CSRM Board Member

"Dr. Linville once again has written a book that provides the SR&F Community with proven pragmatic concepts based in sound Theology. He continues to be a voice crying in the wilderness. Is anybody listening?"

— Tim Conrad
Founder and President of Uncharted Waters / UW Sports Ministry
Author

"When God's word, academia & personal experience all come together within the pages of one book, the SR&F practitioner is all set for both inspiration and revelation. As with his previous books Greg Linville has crafted together the key tenets of Sports Outreach and the great commission with the Universal Church and local congregation in mind. Be ready with your highlight pen; there are some golden phrases coming up."

– Bryan Mason
Founder of Higher Sports
Author & Former CSRM European Director

"As usual Dr. Greg Linville challenges and provokes us winsomely and graciously. No one does it better."

— Rev. Rob Burns
Founding Director, Mission Links Wales
CSRM Staff Emeritus
Former Professional Football (Soccer) Player

"I am grateful this book and the entire book series highlights the important areas of Theology for Ministry."

— Barb Wagenfuhr
Retired Director of Recreational Ministries
Founding Board Member and Past board President – CSRM

"All Sports Ministers wanting to fully understand and evaluate the focus of their ministry must read The Saving of Sports Ministry. The way Dr. Greg speaks about Competition and Salvation has revolutionized the way I lead P4E. ...Where the Focus should be...What are the TRUE goals...and How to evaluate our success are all things this book addresses. I will turn to The Saving of Sports Ministry over and over again to help guide me through this Sports Ministry world."

— **Don Weyrick**
Director and Founder of P4E (Playing 4 Eternity Sports Ministry)
Part of REACH Program Team
Runs one of the top Basketball Leagues in California
Coaches one of the Top Pro Am Teams in California

"Dr. Linville has written yet another powerful must-read and must-have book for anyone seeking to fulfill their call to Sport, Recreation and Fitness Outreach Ministry (SR&F). This remarkable book is written by a man of God whose global vision and intention is equipping the local church to change lives through sports."

— **Susan Stewart**
1996 Olympian
Author of *Unbreakable*
Sports Ministry Coordinator of Praise, Cathedral Worship Center
Missisauga, Ontario

"The Institute of Sports Ministry book series has impacted my life to an extent that I am more eager to empower local churches on the African continent for *Strategically-Relevant* and *Efficiently-Effective Evangelistic-Disciplemaking*. These books gives a clear understanding and explanation to our Multi-Faith African churches. This series provides ministerial insights and biblical truth, history and understanding for all of us in Africa who are starved for knowledge of Sports Ministry. It will also serve as rich resources to better equip leaders throughout our African Continental churches on all the biblical basics that are only now being taught to us Africans."

— **Bradley Barnes**
CSRM Continental Director

PREFACE

Vision For This Book
A Future or a Past?

The current "*Sports Outreach Community*" has had a great past but, its future is uncertain! Why do I say this? A quick perusal of the following realities will reveal disconcerting facts and trends.

First, there is a growing cynicism about the authenticity of the faith of most so-called "Christian Sports Personalities," even within the faith community. When coupled with the western world's increasing secularization and antagonism to Christianity, the Sports Outreach methodology of providing "platforms" for elite athletes to "proclaim" their faith has become less and less strategic, relevant and effective.

This cynicism translates into the lack of effectiveness of traditional Sports Outreach methods. For example, high profile Christian athletes (like a quarterback of a winning Super Bowl team) can still draw a crowd to hear a "gospel testimony," but the sad reality is, such crowds have become increasingly populated with people who already have a faith in Jesus. Whereas even ten years ago, these *Mega-Events* included many unchurched, secularized, non-believers; things have really changed. Other *Proclamation-Platforms* such as books, articles, blogs, podcasts or other media avenues are proving less and less effective due to how Christianity has been marginalized in the western world and beyond. Of course, in many countries, possession of such materials would endanger the very lives of anyone found with them.

Second, and perhaps even more disturbing, is how many congregations have ended, or greatly curtailed their Sports, Recreation and Fitness (SR&F) Outreach Ministries because of the ineffectiveness of "canned" sports programs they have relied upon. The sad reality is most "league/event in a box" or "plug and play," programs have proven to have limited success in producing new disciples, new church members, higher Lord's Day worship attendance or larger financial revenues. Thus, I believe there is a need for this book and for the entire series of books of which this is the fourth. To that end, there are a few basic concepts that need to be addressed to ensure the future of local church SR&F Outreach Ministries that this series of books is attempting to address:

1. Questionable Expectations. I once consulted with a church that was planning to add a "Family Life Center." Overall, the plan was a good one, except for

T I M E O U T

The Sports Outreach Movement
Consists of 4 Main Components:

1. Sports-related, para-ministries focused on elite athletes and coaches such as:
   a. Athletes in Action (AIA)
   b. Ambassadores in Sport (AIS)
   c. Hockey Ministries International (HMI)

2. Sports Chaplaincy Ministries such as:
   a. Baseball Chapel
   b. Motor Racing Outreach
   c. Sports Chaplains Network

3. Camping & Outdoor Ministries such as:
   a. Summer's Best Two Weeks
   b. Camp All America
   c. Shekinah Ranch Camp

4. Local church SR&F Outreach Ministries serviced by groups such as:
   a. The Association of Church & Recreation Ministers (CSRM)
   b. CSO/CEDE
   c. Higher Sports
   d. Impact Basketball
   e. SOLA
   f. Uncharted Waters
   g. Upward

the funding plan. The church was planning to borrow the money for the new athletic facilities and anticipated paying the loan off from the donations they would receive from the people the new facility would bring to the church. They continued on with their plan in spite of the dire warnings presented that included the realization that it normally takes 6-7 years for a totally secularized, non-churched, nonbeliever to become a growing Disciple of Jesus; and moreover, it often takes a few additional years before these new disciples start to tithe! That church experienced a decade-long financial crisis which greatly curtailed their outreach because they frequently needed to rent out their facilities to "paying" groups, often precluding using the new building for outreach ministry.

2. Questionable Focus. Utilizing typical sports-related, para-ministries models have not proven effective in bringing people into the necessary long-term fellowship, teaching, preaching and overall accountability of a local congregation. There is a place and purpose for para-ministry methodology but local congregations have far superior and more effective models available to them for making disciples.

3. Questionable Methodology. As already alluded to, relying on *Platform-Proclamations* of elite athletes and scheduling short-term *Mega-Events* rather than empowering ongoing *Repetitive-Redemptive-Relationships* endeavors bear very little fruit.

4. Questionable Training. Volunteer missionaries (league directors, coaches, referees, fitness instructors) in SR&F Outreach Ministries have need of being mobilized, trained, equipped, mentored and encouraged for SR&F Outreach Ministry. Yes it's helpful if such local church missionaries know the order of the books of the Bible, church history and basic doctrines; but if they cannot lead, play or coach a sport, and interact favorably with people then their effectiveness will be hampered. If they do not understand the athletic culture and/or despise competition, then it really doesn't matter how much of the Bible they know because they will never be able to develop any *Repetitive-Redemptive-Relationship* endeavors that winsomely encourage others to desire to hear about their biblical knowledge or Theological truths.

A Future or a Past?

These examples are the mere "tip of the proverbial iceberg," and represent a few of the many reasons why the so-called *Sports Outreach Movement* (what is referred to in this book series as the *Sports Outreach Community*) is on shaky ground. Thus, this all provides the backdrop to why this book is necessary. If

The Community is to have a future, much change is required including a major refocus of *The Movement's* organizational *Philosophical-Principles* and other foundational concepts.

While a few sports-related, para-ministries and methodologies (see the "Score Board" on page xx) are growing, most are in fact static or even declining. In particular, since 2005 the local church segment of the *Sports Outreach Community* has seen a decline in both churches that offer sports programs and in the numbers of professional local Church-Recreators and Sports Ministers. Why? I believe there are two main *Level #3 Methodological-Model* reasons: a) reliance upon a ministry model of *Personality-over-Presence*; and b) reliance upon a model I describe as *Leading-with-Buildings* rather than *Building-with-Leaders*. The "winds of our world have shifted," but we in *The Sports Outreach Community* have yet to "adjust our sails."

Across the globe, violence to missionaries has risen to a level not seen for centuries, and the increasingly secular media outlets have caused great harm to specific Christian denominations and congregations and to Christianity in general. These "wind shifts" should by themselves make it evident that "sail adjustments" are needed. Yet the relatively youthful, eight-decade-old *Sports Outreach Community* seems oblivious, and has joined the two-millennia-old Church in saying "but we've always done it that way." *Level #3 Methodological-Models* need to adapt! Truly, *The Sports Outreach Community* stands at a crossroad!

Therefore, it is my opinion that the future of *The Sports Outreach Community* depends upon a "sail-adjusted," refocusing. Specifically, *The Community* would be greatly enhanced by adopting a newly perceived organizational structure that I have termed: *The 3-Tier Paradigm*. This new organizational structure will provide foundational, Christo-centric, *Level #1 Theological-Truths*, which inform solid Biblically-based, *Level #2 Philosophical-Principles*; out of which can emerge a re-envisioning and revitalization of a *Level #3 Model* of "equipping the saints." This equipping will include mobilizing them for long-term *Strategically-Relevant* and *Efficiently-Effective*, missiologically-based *Sports Outreach Methodology*.

Specifically the vision for this book is to provide *The Sports Outreach Community* a solid foundation for determining an effective and pragmatic soteriology upon which to build a future that mobilizes congregations to reach those far from Jesus and His Church. It joins previous books and adds to the foundation being laid for future books in this series to build upon.

EXPLANATORY NOTES FOR THE
INSTITUTES OF THE SPORTS OUTREACH COMMUNITY
BOOK SERIES

DISTINCTIVES OF THIS BOOK SERIES

This is the fourth in the "Institutes of Sports Outreach" series of books which will eventually consist of at least 12 distinct works. While each book could stand alone; the entire series is based on, and united through, the overarching organizational structure of the *3-Tier* Paradigm (see book #2). Each book either builds upon, and/or refers to others in the series. A quick review of the previous books include…

• Book #1 ("Christmanship") introduced basic Theological and ethical foundations, which serve as the basic apologetic for Sports Outreach.
• Book #2 ("Sports Outreach Fundamentals") outlined the *Level #2 Philosophical-Principles* that serve as the Biblically-based, organizational structure for ensuring a *Strategically-Relevant* and *Efficiently-Effective* SR&F Outreach.
• Book #3 ("Putting The Church Back Into Church Sports") was the first entry into *Level #1 Theological-Truths* and established ecclesiology as a fundamental Theological foundation for Sports Outreach Ministry.

The series will continue with a number of *Level #1 Theological-Truth* books including missiology and Christology. These books will work together to inform and guide Level #2 *Philosophical-Principles* transferable concepts from which *Level #3 Methodological-Models* will emerge.

The oversight for this series of books includes maintaining: a) a consistent editorial board (made up of a strong group of practitioners, academics and editors); b) a general editor (myself); c) book editors (many secured but unannounced at this time); d) book section editors; and e) book and chapter authors (also not announced at this time). What follows in this and subsequent books is the fulfillment of the plan that emerged from an overall vision, and the distinctive perspective, from which the "Institutes of Sports Outreach" book series was conceived. This all contributes to giving this series of books a unique and catalytic place in propelling Sports Outreach into its 2nd century.

Further distinctions and core values of The Institutes of Sports Outreach include: I. Vision; II. Orthodoxy and Orthopraxy; III. History & Theology; IV. Citations; V. Use of Italics; VI. Thoughts on *The Movement*; VII. Thoughts on the Words Church, Local Church and Congregation; and VIII. Capitalization

EXPLANATORY NOTES FOR THIS BOOK SERIES

I. Vision

This series of books has been envisioned to communicate the *Information of The Sports Outreach Community* for the purpose of resourcing, training, connecting and equipping local church Sports, Recreation & Fitness (SR&F) Outreach Ministers for the end goal of them being able to mobilize, enable and empower their congregations to fulfill the Great Commission. While it is hoped that this series will also prove to be relevant and beneficial for all Sports Outreach endeavors, it is written by and for local church SR&F practitioners.

II. Orthodoxy and Orthopraxy

One of the key distinctions of this series of books has to do with the intentional target of the material presented. This series is designed to be a complementary blend of Orthodoxy and Orthopraxy.

Orthodoxy is a word that is somewhat familiar to most within *The Sports Outreach Community*, as it is a much used term within Christianity that describes true-to-the-Bible Theology and philosophy. However, not everyone would be able to accurately define it, let alone understand its importance and relevance to SR&F Outreach Ministry. If such confusion exists about the word Orthodoxy, then how much more true would it be about the term Orthopraxy, of which most Christians are unfamiliar. Further explanations are helpful.

Orthodoxy and Orthopraxy derive from a common Greek root: "ortho" – which means straight, right, or correct. Thus the straightening concept found in both words communicates such straightening will bring about righteousness and correctness. However, the two words each have differing suffixes which sends this correcting righteousness in two different directions.

The suffix "doxy" stems from another Greek word which means doctrine or belief. Its Greek etymological root word is *dexomai*. *Dexomai* connotes a receiving of someone or something, and thus when put together Orthodoxy means to receive and believe a straight, right and correct word from God. "Doxy" pertains to thinking and thus, Orthodoxy has to do with right and correct doctrinal and Theological thinking.

The suffix for the second word "praxis" stems from yet a third Greek word which means to practice. "Praxis" has to do with action and activity. Thus, Orthopraxy has to do with the essence of acting in straight, right, correct and/or strategically practical ways. Thus, whereas Orthodoxy deals with correct doctrine and Theology, Orthopraxy pertains to right and correct action.

The relevance to Sports Outreach, and to this book, is that any good Orthopraxy *(Level #3 Methodological Models)* is based upon solid Orthodoxy *(Level #1 Theological-Truths* and *Level #2 Philosophical-Principles)*; as explained in many other books in this series. The entire series of books is based upon this

3-Tier Paradigm which envisions solid Theological and theoretical thinking from which *Strategically-Relevant* and *Efficiently-Effective* SR&F Outreach Ministry can emerge.

III. History and Theology

Theology doesn't develop in a historical vacuum. Moreover, Theology shapes history. Thus, an undergirding distinction of this series of books is to highlight historical anecdotes of people, ministries, churches, missions and organizations which will be used to either: a) illustrate Theology; or b) provide living examples of why Theology (or often the lack of it) is important to comprehending and implementing a *Strategically-Relevant* and *Efficiently-Effective* SR&F Outreach Ministry.

Some of the historical references are ancient, from as early as the 1st Century. However, many will be from the past two centuries; including contributions from current practitioners who share their experiences as they engage in creating contemporary history—both shaping Theology as well as being shaped by Theology.

It is envisioned and hoped the linking of the Theological and theoretical with the pragmatic and practical will enhance not only the comprehension of the reader, but more importantly, this combination will inspire catalytic new visions for *Strategically-Relevant* and *Efficiently-Effective* SR&F Outreach.

These historical vignettes appear throughout the books in the form of special "Time Out" pages.

IV. Citations

Direct quotes are always cited as are more general references that are drawn from specific hardcopy or digital sources; as well as personal conversations. However, some statistical data is assumed without direct referential citing due to the nature of current day search engine capability, and/or because no such research exists. With the wonder of the internet, anyone reading this series of books can have the latest data at their fingertips rather than be unduly influenced by out-of-date statistics available at the time of writing. Readers are encouraged to access current trends and research so as to not be unduly, or even wrongly, persuaded by the outdated data that influenced the narratives found in this series of books; some that may well be challenged or disproved by future research. This editorial decision is intentionally offered so as to engage readers in seeking truth, rather than falling into the trap of believing the false truth of outdated statistics. Thus, assuming a book to have an existence far beyond a specific period of time of research, the editors have often opted to not always take the space to provide research data that often becomes out of date within months. However, a quick perusal of the works cited, or any good web-based search would provide any interested reader with the proper references that served to form the basis of an author's assessments and thus be able to make proper assessments of any thesis proposed by authors.

Another problem exists in relationship to citations. *The Sports Outreach Community* is greatly under researched and thus I often make assertions or statements that are based on my experience and insights rather than hard research. Good examples of this occurred earlier in this explanatory note section in regards to the decline of, and problems of, *The Sports Outreach Community*. I fully believe the trend includes: a) many congregations have made cuts in their SR&F Outreach Ministries; b) many sports-related, para-ministries have seen downward trends in their numbers; and c) many universities have dismantled their Sports Ministry programs; and yet, hard research on these is non-existent.

Beyond these citation issues, this series of books include unique categories of citations put forth as various "sidebars/word boxes." All such side bars are original to the authors of the various books, sections or chapters, unless noted otherwise. There are four major categories of side bars: a) Graphs; b) Charts; c) "Scoreboards," and d) "Time Outs." All four have been designed to help the reader contemplate, visualize and implement the content of the narrative. Examples of all four can be found throughout this series of books with the following distinctions.

Graphs show the results of surveys or anything that can be counted and compared. Charts are used to pictorially illustrate the concepts being written about. The third category entitled: "Scoreboards" is used to highlight and/or further emphasize a major phrase or concept found within the narrative, with the thought being the reader is being reminded to "keep score" of the various points being made and/or to score points by applying the data to their own ministry setting. "Time Outs" allow the reader to take a short break from the narrative, to reflect upon an ancient or contemporary historical model or example of what the narrative is describing.

V. Use of Italics

Italics are used wherever words or terms have been repurposed, created or coined by the authors. In addition, italics are also used whenever unique CSRM language is used. This is done for three main reasons. First, italics are used to emphasize the fact that *The Sports Outreach Community* is in need of creating its own language to accurately define, describe and communicate its unique ethos, culture, structure and mission. Therefore, these unique words and phrases are repeatedly italicized. Second, the goal is to not only familiarize the readers with the important transferable concepts put forth in this book series but more to drill the terms and transferable concepts deep into the psyche of the reader; thus the repetitive use of italics. The third reason is to communicate the unique repurposing of words and/or phrases that otherwise might be understood in ways that are different than for which they are utilized in The Community and this book. Italics are also used for all foreign language words.

VI. Thoughts on *The Movement*

The phrase that SR&F Outreach Ministries are often referred to is: *The Sports Outreach Movement*, or simply *The Movement*. At the time of writing, this is the term used by most SR&F leaders. I have however, become increasingly less comfortable with the phrase. This discomfort has to do with the subtle communication that what is done in SR&F Outreach Ministry takes place outside of the traditional body of Christ (The Church), and becomes an entity unto itself (thus a movement) superseding, and existing outside of The Church. In reality this so-called *Movement* is simply one expression of how The Church reaches and incorporates those far from Christ and His Church.

Thus, *The Sports Outreach Movement* terminology has been used throughout the first books of this series but has been changed in this and future editions to the phrase: *Sports Outreach Community*.

VII. Thoughts on the Words: The Church, Local Church and Congregation

The words "The Church" will be used whenever the universal body of Christ is intended, and both words (The and Church) will be capitalized. Whenever a local assembly of The Church is referenced, it will be done so in lower case (church). Thus, terms such as: local church; congregation; and other words such as assembly will not be capitalized. To help communicate this distinction the word congregation will be used most often.

VIII. Capitalization

All words relating to, describing or referencing God will be capitalized. This editorial decision serves to communicate and emphasize the Overwhelming Victory Press (OVP) belief that the triune-God is truly worthy of receiving any and all honor possible. Thus the more commonly capitalized words such as God, Lord, Jesus, Holy Spirit will be joined with any pronouns used to refer to God such as Him, He, His and even at times words that reference God such as Who. Other words that have a foreign language derivative of God such as Theology (from the Greek word for God: Theos) will also be capitalized to further express this honor.

Another special use of capitalization is in reference to the Bible. The words Bible and Biblical, along with phrases such as Word of God, will be capitalized for two reasons. The first is to clearly express the belief and commitment of Overwhelming Victory Press (OVP) to communicate its belief that the Bible is sacred literature; above and beyond all other writings and deserves a place of honor. In a day and age in which the Bible is being attacked, criticized and marginalized, even within much of Christian scholarship, the second reason has to do with communicating OVP's belief and commitment that the Bible is the inerrant, infallible and fully trustworthy Word of God; and that it is fully authoritative for The Church. Capitalization of these words should not however be understood that OVP believes the Bible to be God, but rather His Word.

IX. Co-Authors

Another distinction and core value of Overwhelming Victory Press has to do with the recognition that The Church is made up of a myriad of individual disciples of Jesus. This recognition is exemplified in this book series by each book being co-authored by a number of different people. The way these co-authors integrate their contributions is best described through the metaphor of a sports broadcast.

Most sports broadcasts have at least 3 distinct roles that are needed to fully communicate the events of the game, match or race. The first role is that of the "play-by-play" announcer who gives a running narrative, describing each specific play. The second role is often called the "color analyst" and seeks to enhance the running narrative by elaborating on, and further explaining, the "play-by-play." The "color" man/woman provides additional information by explaining the why, the when and the who involved in a specific play or strategy that worked; or in some cases, why it didn't work. The third role in a broadcast team is usually an on the field reporter who conducts interviews and provides up close and personal insights.

The "broadcast team" assembled for the Institutes of Sport Outreach book series is currently made up of four regular contributing authors and individual cameos by other veterans in the field. The "play-by-play" role is filled by Dr. Greg Linville who provides the basic content and oversees the flow of that content. The "color" and "on the field" roles are filled by three others.

Greg English contributes in many of the chapters a piece entitled: A Practitioner's-Perspective. His role is to take the theory of the "play-by-play" and make it relevant to local church SR&F Outreach Ministers.

P. F. Myers role is to bring an international perspective to the narrative so as to make the data relevant to the *SR&F Outreach Community* throughout the world, and also to enable stateside SR&F Outreach Ministers to benefit and learn from those practitioners in other countries and cultures. Myers's insights can be found throughout the books under the title of: International Insights.

Dr. Vickie Byler joins the broadcast team for the first time in fourth book of the book series. As a long time Professor and a former University department chair, her role is to add academic insights coming from research and also by providing information concerning citations. Byler's contributions are found under the title of: Research Reflections.

In addition to these regular contributing authors, there is a lengthy list of SR&F veterans (guest authors) who contribute invaluable, one-off insights. These essays are most often found in side bars entitled: Time Out.

A Final Word

To revisit and restate the Vision of this series: the laser-focus of this series of books is to enhance and expand the *Evangelistic-Disciplemaking* efforts of individual members and congregations of The Church. This series of books is written by, and for all within, *The Sports Outreach Community* but especially for local church SR&F Outreach Ministers. It is produced by the publishing arm of the Association of Church Sports & Recreation Ministers (CSRM)— Overwhelming Victory Press (OVP)—for all who are called to this most strategic and catalytic outreach of The Church. The prayers of the CSRM staff, Board of Trustees and supporters are that the Lord of the universe will use this series to supernaturally empower all who read this series.

— Dr. Greg Linville – Director of Resource Development CSRM
Author and General Editor for The Institutes of Sports Outreach
From the shores of Lake Erie at Lakeside Chautauqua - 2019

EXPLANATORY NOTES FOR
THE SAVING OF THE SPORTS OUTREACH COMMUNITY
"THE SOTERIOLOGY OF SPORTS OUTREACH"

"I don't know any more about Theology than a jack-rabbit does about
ping-pong, but I'm on the way to glory."
– Billy Sunday

The first book of this Institute of Sports Outreach Book Series (*Christmanship*) established the basic apologetic for Sports Outreach and initiated the process of how Sports Outreach Leaders could think Theologically, organize philosophically and compete ethically. It explained the difference between competition, sport and recreation and proposed a Christian Ethic for the integration of faith and sport.

Book two (*Sports Outreach Fundamentals*) outlined how Sports, Recreation and Fitness (SR&F) Outreach Ministers could envision, plan for and implement a *Strategically-Relevant* and *Efficiently-Effective, Evangelistic-Disciplemaking* Outreach Ministry. That book rests upon this and other *Level #1 Theological-Truth* books of this series.

Book three (*Putting The Church Back In The Game*) was the first in the series that specifically dealt with one of Level #1 Theological-Truths Ologies - Ecclesiology. It made a case for the importance of basing all *Sports Outreach Ministry* in and through a local congregation.

This book (*The Saving of Sports Ministry*) takes another step in establishing the foundational Christo-centric, *Level #1 Theological-Truths* concerning the soteriology (salvation) of The Church as it relates to Sports Outreach. In other words, this book attempts to define and articulate a clear and understandable Theology of salvation (what is called soteriology in Academic circles). It will also suggest the implications of soteriology for determining the organizational structure for *The Sports Outreach Community*.

As general editor of this book series and author of this book, I make two pledges. The first is of primary importance to all of us who have served as SR&F practitioners: I pledge to make every attempt at making what could become a most high-brow and tedious book, relevant and readable. Yet, even with this said, I hope to challenge SR&F practitioners to grow in their Theological comprehension and knowledge, in their ministry ability, and most of all in their relationship with Jesus and His Word. If this book doesn't cause and encourage Theological, ministerial and spiritual growth, then I have failed. I want to meet SR&F Outreach Ministers where they are but motivate them to grow in their knowledge, wisdom and ministry. My hope is also that we will "meet at the train depot," and agree to travel together. My prayer is that we will be courageous enough to get on the train and allow it to take us to the next stops… and that our final destination will be where God wants to grow us.

The second pledge is to the Academy. While I realize this book (and in fact the entire series is not written like, nor does it approximate the kind of academic treatise, article or book that meets typical academic genre, my hope is that true academicians will appreciate the Theological and philosophical bedrock upon which the methodology builds. My prayer is that my academic peers will be supportive of my attempts to build a bridge where academia and ministry can meet, and where orthodoxy shapes orthopraxy and orthopraxy stretches orthodoxy.

My fear is that I will fall short of this goal and please no one, and that academics will deem what I present as Theology light and practitioners will be turned off by weighty language or the occasional complex theory.

This book, *The Saving of Sports Ministry*, is the fourth book in a series projected to include 12 or more total books. This book's specific content is comprised of one sub-set of the *Level #1 Theological Truths* that Sports Outreach is founded on. It has been preceded by, and will be followed by other *Level #1 Theological Truth* books that will collectively outline and discuss how *The Sports Outreach Community* (including local churches) conceptualize, plan for and implement Sports, Recreation and Fitness (SR&F) Outreach Ministry. Such ministries when properly understood and organized in and through *Level #1 Theological-Truths* will not only be relevant and strategic but perhaps even more important, will employ models that effectively reach those far from Christ, and do so with the most efficient utilization of all resources. In fact, when properly conceptualized, (from solid Theological foundations), SR&F Outreach Ministries provide The Church in general, and local congregations in specific with the most powerful methodology The Church has for successful *Evangelistic-Disciplemaking.*

Sadly however, the landscape is strewn with unsuccessful sport and rec programs which have failed because the *Level #3 Methodological Models* were not informed by, conceptualized, planned or implemented in light of the *Level #1 Theological-Truths* which follow in this book and this book series.

The word Theology itself comes from two Greek words: Theos – God; and logos – (where the English word logic comes from); and when put together it actually means a logic (or study) of God. Thus, Theology is a logical study of God. Only when God is fully comprehended can people understand who they are; who they were created to be; and by extension, how local congregations are to conceive of, and implement, their *Evangelistic-Disciplemaking* efforts. What follows in this book is the continuation of a number of introspective looks into the major *Level #1 Theological-Truths* that prove most consistently relevant for envisioning a local church SR&F Outreach Ministry. I refer to them as the *"Ologies"* of *The Sports Outreach Movement.*

DISTINCTIVES OF THIS BOOK

Transferable concepts – All of the transferable concepts outlined in a previous book of this series (*Sports Outreach Fundamentals*) were based upon, and emerge out of what I have termed: *The Ologies of Sports Outreach*, which are the subject of this and subsequent books in this series. I coined the word *"Ologies"* for this series of books to serve as a catch-phrase for foundational *Level #1 Theological-Truths* that undergird and inform the *Level #2 Philosophical-Principles* from which *Level #3 Methodological-Models* emerge. This book and others in this series are what all the transferable concepts found in the previous book (*Sports Outreach Fundamentals*) are based on, formed by and informed by.

Thus, there may be readers of this book that will question the strategic relevance of this book because it consists of more theory and less pragmatics. To those, I would urge holding this book in one hand and the *Fundamentals* book in the other. These Theological foundations are vital to comprehending any effective pragmatic ministry.

Some may then question the order of books. The best way I can explain the order would be to reference Lewis's Narnia series. The story line of the first book of the series (*The Lion, the Witch and the Wardrobe*), was not chronologically the first part of Lewis's mythical history of Narnia. A later book in the series— *The Magician's Nephew*—predated the history of *The Lion, the Witch and the Wardrobe*, and once read, helped make the story line clearer as it connected so many dots. It also had the effect of moving the readers to reread all the previous books in the series; and in doing so, brought an even more significant understanding to the overall message of the author. While I cannot hope to be compared with Lewis's literary skills, it is my hope that this book *The Saving of Sports Ministry* will enable readers to better understand the transferable concepts found in *Sports Outreach Fundamentals*, and thus better be able to envision, plan for and implement a *Strategically-Relevant* and *Efficiently-Effective* SR&F Outreach Ministry.

History and Theology (Mostly Contemporary)—As articulated in the general introduction to this Institute of Sports Outreach Book Series, "Theology doesn't happen in a historical vacuum; and Theology shapes history." Thus, this book continues that tradition in highlighting historical anecdotes of people, ministries, churches, missions and organizations which are used to either illustrate Theology or provide living examples of why Theology (or often the lack of it) is important to comprehending and implementing a *Strategically-Relevant* and *Efficiently-Effective* SR&F Outreach Ministry.

The distinction of this book lies in its historical anecdotes being almost exclusively written by contemporary history makers as they reveal history in the making. These vignettes are found in the various 1-2 page "Time Outs" appearing as highlighted word boxes found throughout the book.

I continue to be much indebted to friends and colleagues who were willing to submit their written contributions for this project. This book has been greatly enhanced by these early 21st century models. This pairing of narrative and contemporary history is probably best understood as a sports broadcast. While the narrative I write is the more mundane "play-by-play" the modern history vignettes written by local church practitioners, are the "color commentators" of the broadcast.

My hope is that the transferable concepts of the previous book will be undergirded by this book in such a way as to create newly proposed working models for the expansion and enhancement of *The Sports Outreach Community's* ultimate goal of world-wide *Evangelistic-Disciplemaking*. It is further hoped the relevance of these transferable concepts will maximize the effectiveness and efficiency of thousands of SR&F Outreach Ministers throughout the world who daily attempt to "go and make disciples."

The *Ologies* found in this and other books in this series are of my own creation stemming from years of directed Bible study and contemplative reflection on my own SR&F experiences. While the general soteriological concepts are millennia old, I believe the application to *The Sports Outreach Community* to be seminal, not only in their conception, but also in how they are defined, explained and expressed. Yet, while I state they have been revealed to or discovered by me, I am quick to indicate that they are truly the product of our *Sports Outreach Community* and I am indebted to many, many people who have journeyed with me through this time of revelation and discovery.

Reasoning Together—A hallmark of the Evangelical Friends has been the practice of "reasoning together" whenever difficult and controversial topics arise. The undergirding premise of belief for this practice has been the realization that due to the fallen nature of humankind, individual Christians often err in maintaining a truly orthodox faith in all areas of doctrine and Theology. It is further believed doctrinal heresies are best understood and overcome by "reasoning together."

"Reasoning together" requires three things: A) Appealing to the Word of God as a final and supreme authority; B) Keeping one's heart warm and one's mind open to the guiding inspiration of the Holy Spirit encapsulated by the Quaker concept called the "Inner Light;" and C) Engaging in "civil conversations" with spiritual brethren based on the Holy Spirit's empowerment and enlightenment of the holy scripture.

A. Appealing to the Word of God as a Final and Supreme Authority

The Evangelical Friends join all Protestant traditions who have historically agreed that the Bible is the source and final authority from which all Theological doctrines and ethical mandates are based. More to the point, unless the Word of God is given its proper place as the final authority in all faith and practice matters, arriving at an agreed upon, God-inspired, Theological consensus is impossible. Thus, all "reasoning together" is based on determining a correct interpretation of the Bible which becomes the foundation for all Christo-centric, *Theological-Truths* and those truths then inform the formation of Biblically-based, *Philosophical-Principles* which are to be applied to everyday life. This may all sound well and good, but even a cursory survey of Church history reveals acrimonious, heated and even violent Theological debates raged throughout the last two millennia. This is where the second pre-requisite of keeping hearts warm and minds open becomes so relevant and necessary.

B. Keeping Warm Hearts and Open Minds

I contend the major reason Theological dialogues turn ugly has to do with the heart and minds of those involved. A most important clarifying question has to do with what motivates those in the dialogue: "Do I desire to understand and be convinced of God's Theology; or do I want to convince others of my Theology?!"

Assuming that all involved in Theological dialogues seek God's truth, not political propaganda or ecclesiastical agenda, it behooves all involved to keep their hearts warm to both the Holy Spirit's guidance and their minds open to the "reasonings" of their spiritual brethren. It stands to "reason" that no human possesses a perfect Theology. Thus logically, we need one another to come to a Spirit led consensus on what a proper Theology is. Furthermore, we only hurt ourselves if we are unwilling to open our hearts and minds to the Holy Spirit speaking to us through the hearts and minds of our brothers and sisters in the Lord. This can only happen by engaging in Civil Conversation.

C. Engaging Spiritual Brethren in Civil Conversation

This third pre-requisite for "reasoning together" is often the most difficult to achieve; in fact it is nearly impossible to arrive at any consensus about a proper Theology if hearts are cold and minds are closed. Furthermore, civil conversations cannot occur unless all conversants honor, love and respect those whom they are engaged with in such conversations—even those whom they vehemently disagree with because they are so deeply repulsed by the other's views.

Nonetheless, through the centuries, when the three pre-requisites are met that enable such open, honest, direct and deliberate discourses, followers of Jesus have experienced "God's Theology" and achieved consensus.

It is in that spirit that I enter into a civil conversation about the soteriology of *The Sports Outreach Community*—especially in chapters 6-9. If what I propose here and elsewhere is Theologically sound, then my hope would be that it would convince others who prior to this "reasoning together" may have believed otherwise. Of course, if what I propose here is in error, then I pray my heart would remain warm to Jesus and my mind would be open to clearer thinking, with the end goal of not insisting on my Theology, but rather attaining Jesus's Theology through our *Sports Ministry Community* collectively and collaboratively coming to consensus.

Citations

There are two general differences in citations for this book than for previous books in this series: 1) The work of a new co-author; 2) Citations concerning the Great Commission.

Co-Author—With this book we welcome a new contributing author—Dr. Vickie Byler. Dr. Byler has a strong Sports Ministry and academic pedigree that includes both a passion and ability for research and critical thinking. Her contributions will center on linking readers to relevant sources. While OVP's editorial policy of relying on readers to "fact check" many individual statements throughout the narrative of the books (see the Institutes of Sports Outreach Book Series Explanatory Notes), part of Dr. Byler's role as co-author lies in providing readers with additional links to resources and data.

The Great Commission—Due to the nature and topic of this particular book, the Great Commission passage of Matthew 28.19, 20 will not be officially cited with a footnote each time it is referenced. This decision is based on the best stewardship of time, space and effort on the part of authors, editors, graphic artists, printers and of course readers. It will be cited in the actual narrative throughout the manuscript by actually spelling out the words "Great Commission" or by simply incorporating any of the following: "go;" "going;" "go into all the world;" "go to make disciples;" "disciplemaking" etc. Citing the Great Commission in this way actually serves to give Jesus command to go into all the world and make disciples it's well deserved preeminence as the one major reference for the entire book. For official citation purposes, The Great Commission passage is offered just below...

"Go therefore and make disciples of all nations, baptizing them in the name of the Father and of the Son and of the Holy Spirit, teaching them to observe all that I have commanded you. And behold, I am with you always, to the end of the age." Matthew 28.19, 20

Final Words

May this book be used of the Lord to *Inform, Instruct and Inspire* all within *The Sports Outreach Community* to engage, equip and empower their church to reach those who are far from Jesus and His Church.

— Dr. Greg Linville – Director of Resource Development CSRM
Author and General Editor for The Institutes of Sports Outreach
From the shores of Lake Erie at Lakeside Chautauqua - 2019

ACKNOWLEDGEMENTS

GENERAL ACKNOWLEDGEMENTS

How can you ever adequately acknowledge all those who have impacted you? I very much see this book, and this entire series of books, as only being possible because of the myriad of people who have influenced and inspired me. While I find it difficult to always identify exactly when and where one idea or person inspired another, and similarly, it is often hard to know who inspired whom. What's easier to say is I know I owe much, to many! To that end, I acknowledge that this book is a true synthesis of many influence of my life. Thus, to all who are cited here, and many others, I say again thank you for your part in making this book a reality!

As always, though much credit should go to others for all that is true and positive in this work; I remain completely responsible for any flaws or shortcomings presented; and in no way wish to suggest any of my errors in reasoning, remembering, or hermeneutics, are the fault of any of my colleagues. In addition, if I have not given adequate or appropriate credit to anyone for their influence, I would humbly ask to bring this oversight to my attention so I can apologize and give proper acknowledgement in future editions.

It should also be noted that much of the content of this book can be found in various articles, chapters, blogs, videos, lectures presentations and treatises I have produced over the years. Nonetheless what appears here originated with me except where noted. One specific example of this was revealed when our editorial board used a digital checker on my previous work and found that some 17 percent of what I had written had come from other sources! They were relieved to find that over 90% of those sources not cited were of my own previous writings.

SPECIFIC ACKNOWLEDGEMENTS
Thanks to all Co-Authors:
Guest Authors – those who contributed one specific essay

Chris Phillips - Chris led one of the premier local church SR&F Outreach Ministry for many years; is one of the keenest minds and clearest thinkers of the entire SR&F Outreach Community; and is currently planting a church using the very principles espoused in this series of books. Chris's winsome and contagious spirit is only surpassed by his commitment to Gospel-centered ministry and love for his family. I am blessed to be able to call Chris friend.

ACKNOWLEDGEMENTS

Bob Schindler – There are few people who I have worked more closely with or who I appreciate more than Bob. Bob is one of the most beloved and respected people in the entire *Sports Outreach Community*. Our shared experiences and partnership have enabled me to witness Bob's true character and commitment and I can affirm that there is no one with whom I have worked who has a higher or deeper level of character and commitment. I thoroughly enjoy our shared experiences in equipping, empowering and inspiring local church sports ministers.

Stuart Weir – When the history books are written Stuart will be considered one of the most influential people in the entire *Sports Outreach Community*. A former staff member of Christians in Sport and the current Director of Verite' Sport, Stuart is known throughout the sporting world in his role of supporting athletes the world over and he is perhaps *The Community*'s most prolific author having nearly a score of books to his credit. His ongoing, online, list of Sports Ministry references and book reviews provides an incomparable resource and his innate and intuitive insights are valued by anyone who knows him. It is a privilege to count him as friend and partner.

Contributing Authors

This entire book series would not be nearly as significant without three ongoing, regular contributing authors; all whom are credited at length in the Explanatory Note Frontispiece of this book. I would be remiss however if I didn't thank each of them here by name: Dr. Vickie Byler; P. F. Myers and Greg English. Thanks to each of you.

Thanks to the Overwhelming Victory Team

Thanks to OVP's Editorial Board who took the time to read through the manuscript; affirming where warranted; and critiquing where needed. This editorial team includes: Dr. Vickie Byler; Doug Cassady; Greg English; John Garner; Dr. Jimmy Smith; Dr. Stan Terhune; David Waddell and Dr. Steven Waller; ... all whom provided great critique and much needed editing.

Thanks to those who take the manuscript and work their magic. This team includes:

Wendy Satterwhite, our graphic artist who creates all book covers and continues to take all the rough draft manuscripts and turn them into an amazing final draft suitable for going to print.

Gordon Theissen, who is the official printer (Cross Training Publishing) for

ACKNOWLEDGEMENTS

Overwhelming Victory Press and produces such wonderful print versions of each book.

Stan Terhune who is our final editor and is greatly responsible for making sure every "t" is crossed, every punctuation point is in place and every citation is correctly aligned.

CONCLUDING ACKNOWLEDGMENTS

Acknowledging Those Previously Cited I want to communicate to all who have been cited more fully in my previous books that you have also impacted this book either through your original influence that helped set the course for this entire series of books or through your continuing insights and support. Although I won't take the space to once again outline your catalytic role in my life, thinking and mission, I will state once more that this book and the entire series would not exist without your unique contribution to my thinking, my experiences and my life in general. Although not specifically cited by name here...I remain indebted to each person acknowledged in previous books: thank you!

A number of additional special people also bear special mention... My family: I continue to thank God for my Grandparents and parents who prayed for and counseled me throughout life. In addition my wife, children and their spouses who continue to support and encourage me, and without whom, none of these books would ever be written. Also to my grandchildren who are a constant joy and who now are participating in local church sports leagues and camps. I write with a hope that this book will help to ensure you and your generation a sporting future through a local church that will bring salvation to each of you.

CSRM: This book also would not have come to print without the ever growing and expanding CSRM family. Each current and former Board and staff member played a role in this book being published. A special thanks to Kat Linhart who handles all of the order taking, shipping and processing of all book orders.

First Friends Church: Not only is this book greatly dependent upon what has been collectively learned through the SR&F Outreach Ministry at First Friends Church, but the ongoing support of the First Friends family continues to be expressed in dedicated prayer and financial assistance is foundational to the publication of this book. Even as this book was being written the church blessed me with the opportunity to continue as a leader in the Sports Ministry in both the adult men's open basketball league and the basketball clinic that my 5 and 6 year grandsons participated in!

FINAL WORDS

To each of you who have had an impact or an influence on my life and thinking, I say thank you. I recognize this to be much more God's work than mine; a true Kingdom effort. I have felt a weight of responsibility to undertake the exhausting effort to bring it all together in an attempt to further expand and enhance His Church; rather than my personal portfolio. It is to His glory and for the purpose of redeeming the people of sport as well as redeeming the world of sport that I write.

Chapter 1

Review of Previous Books in the AGON Institutes of Sports Outreach Series

I. Introduction - Where are We? Where are We Going?

This is the fourth book in the Institutes of Sports Outreach Book Series. The entire series is envisioned from, organized by, and follows, the structure of *The 3-Tier Paradigm*. It establishes the second of *The Sports Outreach Ologies* that serve as the Theological foundation for the entire book series, and portions of the first chapter of the previous book are incorporated into this chapter. This look back at previous books is primarily for the purpose of bringing new readers of this series up to date, although readers of the previous books may appreciate a brief review of the former material. However, the even more significant purpose of this chapter is the ever-so-short look forward as to the overall purpose for why this specific book is necessary… the woeful state of The Church's current *Evangelistic-Disciplemaking* efforts.

A. The Current View

A sad reality is occurring in many North American congregations. Local church leaders are asking the hard question:

"Why isn't our church growing? Something doesn't make sense because we hear almost every week about people who are making decisions for Christ in our sports leagues and yet our church isn't growing!"

Do you often ask the same question? Does your SR&F Outreach Ministry keep track of how many "salvations" occur as a result of your outreach efforts? If so, is there a direct correlation to your congregation growing? If not, how do you resolve this disconnect between the number of "salvations" and lack of church growth? Beyond your congregation, the world situation of The Church also reveals the same disturbing trends.

The websites of contemporary missions, ministries and churches celebrate how many "salvations" their efforts have witnessed, and if these statistics are to be believed, it would seem the entire world is in the midst of revival. Certainly, there are places in the world where revival is occurring, yet the overall question remains: on the whole, why are global congregational numbers dwindling? Yes, Scripture assures that God is consistently and constantly at work in fulfilling what Jesus said: "I came to seek and save the lost." However, despite the occasional encouraging report of specific regions experiencing revival, it is troubling to know The Church is in decline in many countries where it once was the dominate influence of the entire culture, and it is being persecuted into oblivion in regions where it had long flourished!

Beyond the faltering of the Western Church and the oppressive persecution of Christians from other faith traditions throughout the world, could it be that the nature of the pervasive social media culture has played a role in making it seem there have been more "salvations" in our lifetime than ever before. By creating an ever expanding sort of "fake news" through the re-postings, retweets and other digital platforms for spreading such reports, has the Church gotten lazy in its evangelism because it is caught up in a hoped-for and hyped-up expectation rather than maintaining a more reasoned and accurate reality?

Another question that is raised in this book has to do with: what is being counted; what is actually being assessed. I contend that one of the main reasons for the disconnect between the reports of the millions of "salvations" and the shrinking of congregational attendance and membership numbers comes down to what is meant by the word salvation. Furthermore, my contention has to do with the fact that what is being counted doesn't accurately communicate what the hoped for reality is. In other words, if the reported numbers of "salvations" that ministries, missions and churches report reflect the number of people who raised a hand at a particular outreach (*Days-Decisions*), that is something much different than reporting the numbers of *Dedicated-Disciples* that were "made" as a result of evangelistic endeavors.

Regardless, the root cause of these questions and confusions stem from what is, at best, an under-developed Theology of salvation (soteriology) and at worse, it emerges from a heretical view of the same. *The SR&F Outreach Community* is in need of a solid Theology of salvation from which it can envision, plan for, administrate and expedite endeavors that meet the *4-Fold Evaluative Rubric*.

Should we be concerned? Should *The Sports Outreach Community* care? I thought so, that's why I wrote this book!

II. Review of the Books in the Series

As a previous book in this series stated:

"GPS has made maps a thing of the past. Call me old school, but no matter how sweet the digital voice sounds, I find a map to be much more helpful. Why? At a glance, maps not only tell you when and where to turn, they also show where you are, how you got there, and provide all kinds of options for where you could go—and whether you want to take the circuitous scenic route or the lickety-split super highway. This chapter serves as a kind of a map, in that it recaps where we've been and how we got there. Where we can go is the topic for the next chapter. However, before we proceed, the following needs to be reviewed."

A. Review of Book #1 - *Christmanship*

Christmanship was a seminal work that explored the Theology and philosophy of the integration of faith and sport. It was designed as an apologetic for Biblical sport and Christ-honoring ethic for participation in sport. It included the following.

SCOREBOARD

Day's Decision or Dedicated Disciple – #2

A conversation with a friend who was a state director for a prominent sports-related, para-ministry confirmed the importance of rooting coaches and athletes in a Bible-based congregation.

My friend heard me talking about the need to get athletes and coaches intimately involved in a local church and he challenged me! He said it wasn't good enough to get players to become part of just any church because in his experience, unless Christian athletes became involved with a solid Bible-teaching and Christ-honoring body of believers who took "making disciples" seriously, their faith was doomed to become ship-wrecked.

How's your sports-related, para-ministry doing in this regard? Is your local church SR&F Outreach Ministry really connecting those who participate in your outreach activities with the discipling activities of your church?

1. Philosophical and Theological Foundations for Competition and Sport

The first chapter of *Christmanship* defined and outlined The *Progressive Intensity Levels* (PIL) of Competition, the *Internal Motivational Influences of Competition* (IMIC); the *External Motivational Influences of Competition* (EMIC); and explained how they all fit together to create the *Volatility Scale* of sport.

The second chapter explored the Theological foundation for competition based on both Divine and natural revelation and explained competition as perceived from the Theological rubric of: "creation, fall and redemption."

2. Principles for Determining Biblical, Christ-honoring Sport

Chapter three outlined the Biblical principles for determining which sports could be considered Christ-honoring. Chapter four provided the criteria for determining which specific sports could be considered Biblically defensible.

3. Historic Models of Biblical Sport

Chapter five provided a historical overview of how the Church in general and Christians specifically have integrated faith and sport. It included a seminal view of the four classic ways Christians approached sport and competed. It also provided an overview of the Muscular Christianity era.

4. A Christian Ethic of Competition

Chapter six consisted of a detailed Christian ethic of how to compete and engage in sport. It included a comparison of Gamesmanship, Sportsmanship and Christmanship.

5. Frequently Asked Questions About Sport Including Sport & the Lord's Day

Chapters seven and eight addressed many common ethical dilemmas faced by Christian sportspeople. These included Lord's Day issues and sport participation; violence in sport; worship and sport; the value of sport/fitness; and would Jesus commit a foul! One keenly important section included an expository study on the troubling verse that is often used to teach that sport and physical exercises are of no value (1Timothy 4.8).

B. Review of the book: "Sports Outreach Fundamentals - The Transferable Concepts of SR&F Outreach Ministry"

The second book in the AGON Institutes of Sports Outreach is an explanation of the major *Level #2 Philosophical-Principles* of SR&F Outreach Ministry. These transferable concepts interconnect and build on one another. Collectively, they make up the organizational structure for The *Sports Outreach Community* that truly fulfills the Great Commission of going and making disciples. What follows is a succinct statement about each of the transferable concepts of SR&F Outreach Ministry. They are transferable because they can be transferred to any culture, geographic area, denomination or climate. They are concepts because they are overarching philosophical themes rather than specific outreach activities.

1. The *Evangelistic-Disciplemaking* Mandate

The first transferable concept and the guiding principle of SR&F Outreach is the *Evangelistic-Disciplemaking Mandate*. It describes the end goal of SR&F Outreach Ministry: the making of *Dedicated-Disciples* of Jesus Christ.

2. The *2-Dysconnects of SR&F Outreach Ministry*

The second transferable concept describes and defines the two hurdles SR&F Outreach Ministries encounter in reaching those far from Jesus and His Church. The first is attracting people from the general community in which they live, to the specific local church SR&F community. The second has to do with moving people from the SR&F activities to the broader congregational activities including becoming active participants in traditional worship and Christian education opportunities.

3. The 3-Tier Paradigm

The third transferable concept outlines the organizational structure of SR&F Outreach Ministries. Based upon three levels, it builds from a foundation of how to think/what to believe (Theologically); which shapes and informs how to organize (philosophically); out of which *What* to do (methodology) emerges. Moving from *Why* a SR&F Outreach Ministry exists, to *When*, *Where* and for *Whom* the SR&F is organized, to *What* the SR&F Outreach Ministry actually does; this organizational structure ensures *Strategically-Relevant* and *Efficiently-Effective* *SR&F Outreach Ministry*.

4. The 4-Fold Evaluative Rubric

The fourth transferable concept describes the four necessary components for ensuring a SR&F Outreach Ministry will accomplish its goals and objectives which include being strategic; relevant; efficient and effective.

5. The 5-B's of SR&F Outreach Ministry

The fifth transferable concept explains the process of developing a *Repetitive-Redemptive-Relational* ethos and culture within the SR&F Outreach Ministry for the purpose of making *Dedicated-Disciples* of Jesus. It outlines how SR&F leaders can envision, plan for, organize, administrate and implement an effective outreach ministry. The 5-B's are: *Belong; Believe; Baptize; Behave; Become.*

6. The 7- Sports Outreach Continuums

The sixth transferable concept outlines the seven most important Theological and philosophical issues confronting *The Sports Outreach Community* as it enters its 8th decade.

C. Review of Book #3 – *Putting The Church Back In The Game*

1. Section #1 – Overview and Review

This section serves as the orientation point of the third book, explaining how it fits within the overall narrative of the AGON Institutes of Sports Outreach Book Series and how the book completes the next step of that journey.

2. Section #2 –The Theology of The Church

This section communicates the rationale for why ecclesiology is important to and for *The Sports Outreach Community* and explains its relationship to that community. It also defines the purpose and function of the overall Church and its local congregations in relationship to SR&F Outreach Ministry.

3. Section #3 – Ecclesiastical SR&F Sub-Topics

Section three discusses ecclesiastical topics such as: a) how to envision integrating sport with personal faith and church activities; b) congregational funding of both the local congregation and the congregation's SR&F Outreach Ministry; c) Church leadership; and d) worship. All of these are considered in relationship to SR&F Outreach Ministries.

4. Section #4 – Relevance of Ecclesiology for the SR&F Community

Section four not only reviews the book but more importantly connects many of the sub points into a unified whole that enables congregational leaders and SR&F Outreach Ministers to establish ecclesiastical foundations that truly empower *Evangelistic-Disciplemaking*.

III. Summary of the Review

So far in this AGON Institutes of Sports Outreach Book Series we have established: a) a basic Theological and pragmatic apologetic for competition; b) a Biblical defense for both sport in general and most individual sports; c) an ethical model for Christian engagement in and with competition and sport; and d) six transferable concepts for how to organize SR&F Outreach Ministries according to Biblically-based, *Level #2 Philosophical-Principles*. We also articulated the first of a number of *Sports Outreach Ologies* that undergird Sports Outreach: ecclesiology. Now it's time to tackle the second *Ology*: soteriology – the Theology of salvation. Soteriology is one of the most important *Level #1 Theological-Truths* that serve as the foundation for everything that makes up this series. The next chapter will provide the specific route we will take as our journey continues.

Preview of
The Saving of The Sports Outreach Community: Soteriology
Where We're Headed

I. Introduction – What this book and chapter are about and where they are headed

Have you ever wondered why your congregation is not growing numerically? Many congregational leaders are baffled by conflicting data. On the one hand they report dozens, scores and perhaps even hundreds of individuals who profess faith in Jesus each year through their Sports, Recreation and Fitness (SR&F) Outreach Ministry. As great as this may be, it doesn't seem to increase the number of people attending Lord's Day worship services, nor does it swell the ranks of church membership. Something doesn't add up.

Have you ever struggled with why conversions to Jesus that occur in your Sports Outreach Ministry don't seem to translate into the making of disciples? It may well be, your ministry is not fully aligned with core *Level #1 Theological-Truths*, or built on a Biblically-based, *Level #2 Philosophical-Principles* organizational-structure!

Sadly, soon after church leaders realize congregational numbers are not growing they begin to doubt the effectiveness of SR&F Outreach Ministry. When combined with the need to tighten up budgets, hard decisions are made that often include curtailing or eliminating the congregation's SR&F Outreach Ministry.

Yes, conventional wisdom would seem to say the only way to keep paying

SCOREBOARD

"At first, our congregation rejoiced when we heard about a dozen high school basketball league participants who 'accepted Jesus.'

We were further encouraged when we received the report that 50 summer soccer campers raised their hand to 'get saved.'

We praised God for the end of the year report that indicated that more than a hundred people who were involved in our church's SR&F Outreach activities prayed a 'salvation prayer.'

However, when we assessed the attendance of our Lord's Day Morning services, we realized our numbers had plateaued and perhaps had even gone retrograde. So, we began to ask ourselves the question: 'How can our weekly worship attendance and congregational membership be on a downward trend after having hundreds, if not thousands, of decisions for Christ occur in our Sports Ministry?'"

— *An Elder at "First Church"*

Senior Pastors and/or other Pastoral Staff is to lay off the Sports Pastor! This "knee-jerk" reaction is certainly understandable but incredibly short-sighted.

Hopefully, this book will shed light on this and other issues congregations experience in regards to SR&F Outreach Ministry. Its goal is to provide insight on how to re-envision outreach efforts so they can truly be not only *Strategically-Relevant*, but more important, *Efficiently-Effective*. The ultimate purpose of this book is to aid congregations in their efforts to reach those far from Jesus and His Church.

The *"Ology"* dealing with salvation (soteriology) discussed in this book is a *Level #1 Theological Truth of The 3-Tier Paradigm* as introduced in the third chapter of The Fundamentals of Sports Outreach book. It is one of the core Sport Outreach *"Ologies"* that serve as the foundations which inform and guide the organization of *Level #2 Philosophical Principles*. Soteriology is perhaps the most misunderstood *"Ology"* by *The Sports Outreach Movement*. It is certainly one of the most important! So then, what follows in this book seeks to provide pragmatic answers for such dilemmas.

This chapter explains how Sport, Recreation and Fitness (SR&F) Outreach Ministers can interact with the Theological foundations discussed in this book so as to learn about, and apply the foundations in ways that will enhance and expand their efforts to reach those far from Jesus and His Church.

This book defines, describes and explains one of the most misunderstood Theologies in regards to sports outreach which is the second *Sport Outreach Ology*: soteriology (the Theology of salvation). It was preceded and is followed by other *Ologies* such as ecclesiology, missiology and Christology. When taken as a complete whole, the books in this series that focus on the Theological underpinnings of Sports Outreach provide the basis from which to build an effective and successful SR&F Outreach.

Individually, this book is a *Level #1 Theological-Truth* of the *"3-Tier Paradigm"* (introduced in the third chapter of a previous book in this AGON Institutes of Sports Outreach Book Series: *Sports Outreach Fundamentals*). It deals specifically with how *The Sports Outreach Community* views, engages with, and envisions its collective *Evangelistic-Disciplemaking* efforts.

Collectively, the *Sports Outreach Ologies* provide foundational Level #1 *Theological-Truths* that undergird answers to such pragmatic questions as: Sunday sport; worship and sport; Church and sport; Sports Outreach leadership criteria in relationship to gender and human sexuality issues; effective *Evangelistic-Disciplemaking* strategies; the purpose and role of sports-related, para-ministries and other "sticky" issues experienced by SR&F Outreach Ministers.

II. Vision for this Book

The **Vision** for this book is to see congregations around the world successfully fulfilling their Great Commission Mandate of "going" and "making disciples." The desire of local churches to bring all within their influence into a saving relationship with the Savior Jesus Christ is highly commendable. However, the question must be asked: What does bringing people to faith in Christ entail, and what does getting a person "saved" really mean? Perhaps what's even more important is what this means for local church SR&F Outreach Ministry and the overall *Sports Outreach Community*. Regardless, the bottom line question has to do with the Theology of salvation (soteriology).

There is a prevalent belief that getting someone "saved" means having a person do, or receive one, (or perhaps all of the following): a) come forward at a church service; b) pray "the sinner's prayer;" c) fill out a card at the end of a crusade; d) be baptized; e) become a member of a local church. There is also confusion about "salvation" in relationship to such things as church attendance, tithing, witnessing and other "required" spiritual disciplines. It also begs the question about the relationship between evangelism and discipleship.

How the *Sports Outreach Community* answers the question of what getting a person "saved" means, will directly impact how they envision, plan for and engage in their Great Commission endeavors. How they answer this *Level #1 Theological-Truth* question, determines their *Level #2 Philosophical-Principles* organizational structure, from which their missional *Level #3 Methodological-Models emerge.*

Therefore, this chapter is designed to help all Sport, Recreation and Fitness (SR&F) Outreach Ministers know why and how understanding the Theology of salvation can empower their efforts to mobilize their congregation for *Strategically-Relevant* and *Efficiently-Effective* outreach to people who are far from Jesus and His Church. It is also hoped the broader *Sports Outreach Community* will benefit from what follows so as to enhance and expand their effectiveness in reaching those far from Jesus and His Church.

III. The Mission for this Book

The **mission** of this book is to *Inform The Sports Outreach Community* about the key doctrinal and pragmatic issues issues concerning "making disciples," as it specifically relates to how they envision salvation, evangelism and discipleship; and subsequently how they organize and carry out their outreaches.

This mission is accomplished in this book by both defining soteriology and exploring how to relate it to both the local church SR&F Outreach Ministry and the broader *Sports Outreach Community*. It is hoped this broader community as expressed in sports-focused, para-ministries, camps and chaplaincies will be able to re-evaluate the very Theological foundations their outreaches operate on. The Mission also includes providing the Biblical basis for developing the Theological foundations upon which SR&F Outreach Ministry are based.

Yet, perhaps the most relevant chapter in this book has to do with how to conceptualize contemporary SR&F Outreach Ministry in light of a multi-faith world and the ever increasing secularization of many former Judeo-Christian cultures. Whether it has to do with dealing with the reality that at times Muslims pretend to convert to Christianity only so as to cover their evil intent of spying on a congregation; or a sports-focused, para-ministry is denied access to a college or high school campus unless they adhere to prevailing social mores; *The Sports Outreach Community* is sailing in uncharted waters. In the midst of this, it is hoped this book will help *The Sports Outreach Community* better accomplish its Great Commission goals.

For all of these and other reasons, this book is written. It is offered not so much as "end-all" Theological statement, but more so as a beginning treatise upon which other and deeper conversations can start. Again, the **mission** of this book is to catalytically bring into reality its **vision** to see congregations around the world successfully fulfilling their Great Commission Mandate of "going" and "making disciples." May God add His blessings to this endeavor.

IV. Section by Section Overview
A. Section #2 – The Theological, Philosophical and Biblical Basis of Soteriology

This section will focus on three main areas. The first chapter in this section (Chapter #3) will provide the rationale for why establishing a Theology of salvation is vital to SR&F Outreach Ministry. The next chapter (Chapter #4) will build on the definition of soteriology in general, most specifically in relationship to SR&F Outreach Ministry. The third (Chapter #5) will provide the Biblical basis for establishing a Theology of salvation for SR&F Outreach Ministry.

B. Section #3 – Soteriological Sub-Topics for The Sports Outreach Community

The third section of this book begins the process of applying the Theology (*Level #1 Theological-Truths*) of salvation to the organizational structure of SR&F Outreach Ministry (*Level #2 Philosophical-Principles*) by outlining how to envision, plan for, organize, administrate and implement a *Strategically-Relevant* and *Efficiently-Effective* ministry to those far from Jesus and His Church.

It does so in Chapter #6 by discussing how soteriology is relevant for local church SR&F Outreach Ministry and then Chapters #7 and #8 expands that relevance into the realms of sports-related, para-ministries; camps; and sports-related, chaplaincy-based, ministries.

Perhaps the most relevant chapter in this section is Chapter #9 in that it provides an introspective look at how comprehending soteriology will greatly enable and empower *The Sports Outreach Community* to understand, engage with and reach, those living in a multi-faith world. Soteriology has never been more important to reaching a world so far from Jesus and His Church; especially a world that is increasingly antagonistic to Christianity.

C. Section #4 – Relevancy of Soteriology for *The Sports Outreach Community*

Section four will work to synthesize the first three sections, attempting to "connect all the dots" and offer a few concluding points. In addition it will introduce the *Ology* of the next book in the Institute of Sports Outreach Book Series—missiology.

Rationale for Soteriology in Relationship to SR&F Outreach Ministry

I. Definition of Soteriology

Soteriology is the specific area of Christian Theology that considers salvation; what it means, how it is received and how it is to be understood.

Soteriology includes examining the teaching of the entire bible in relationship to God's work of: a) Planning salvation in the pre-human eternity-past; b) producing salvation in the eternity-present of human history; and c) persevering salvation through all eternity-future for those who are saved.

Therefore, in terms of the salvation of individual people, soteriology is both present and future. It is realized the moment a person makes a *Day's-Decision* and accepts Jesus as Lord and Savior; it continues and is brought to maturity as the new believer learns how to think, act and live as a *Dedicated-Disciple* of Jesus. Finally it is consummated in a heavenly eternity in the very presence of the triune God.

The word soteriology is derived from the Greek word *soter* that means salvation/Savior. It carries the concepts of saving, safety, deliverance, wellness and even healing, but it cannot be boiled down to only one of these concepts, nor can it be demeaned by reducing it to encompass only an earthly relevance of one or more of these concepts. While the understanding of its meaning can be enhanced by considering each of these descriptive words, when used to describe the Theology of salvation, soteriology is specifically dealing with the work of God to regenerate and redeem individuals. This major Biblical doctrine includes and assumes things such as propitiation; expiation; repentance, forgiveness, reconciliation, restoration, justification, sanctification and finally glorification.

Soteriology begins with the work of God (Jesus), Who came to seek and save those who were lost and so enables a person to receive this wonderful gift through faith and who is subsequently indwelt and empowered by the Holy Spirit.

The major distinction of Christian soteriology from other world religions has to do with the fact that it is based on what God has done for humankind, not what humankind does to earn God's love and forgiveness. The very bedrock of Christian soteriology is that nothing a person does can earn salvation; rather it is based solely on what Christ did.

So, what has any of this to do with SR&F Outreach Ministry; why does Soteriology Matter? Read on…

II. Why Soteriology Matters Revisited—Connecting SR&F Outreach Soteriology to *Strategically-Relevant* and *Efficiently-Effective* Level #3 Methodological-Models

I can just hear many of my friends and fellow Sports Ministers! "Seriously Linville? Another book based on another word I can't pronounce? Don't tell me … it's Greek isn't it?"

For those of you who don't know me or have recently joined our *Sports Outreach Community* and have somehow stumbled upon this book, you may not fully understand the good natured "ribbing" that occurs amongst our community. Many of the conversations between me, local church Sports Ministers and University Professors go something like this:

Me: "Soteriology is the most important Theological issue SR&F Outreach Ministry faces today."

My local-church-practitioner partner: "Okay Doc, I'm sure there's something here I need to know and understand but please put it in words that I can understand."

My University associate: "What research is all of this based on?"

So, let me attempt to communicate to both wings of our community: clear and simple, it's about successfully navigating the turbulent waters of bringing people into a personal relationship with Jesus with the end goal of "making Disciples"!

Perhaps said more obtusely—this book is about Gospel-centric, *Evangelistic-Disciplemaking*. It's about communicating why SR&F Outreach Ministers, other

Research Reflections

According to Barna Research, in response to: "The question of how often, and how well, are churches engaging in service and evangelism to their communities," the average number of service projects a church conducted a year was 5. When asked "Is it working?" a majority of pastors report that their church is just somewhat effective. Of those who responded, 13% stated they were very effective, 50% somewhat effective, 32% not very effective and 4% not effective at all.

Despite this, Pastors feel mostly optimistic about their church's efforts in discipleship and spiritual formation: "14% very effective, 73% somewhat effective, 12% not very effective and 1% not effective at all"

Barna Trends 2018: The Truth About a Post-truth Society. Grand Rapids, MI: Baker Books, 2017

— *Dr. Vickie Byler*
Lancaster Bible College

congregational leaders, sports-related camps and sports-oriented, para-ministries need to have a solid soteriology (Theology of salvation). It is designed so they can envision, plan for, organize, administrate and implement a SR&F Outreach Ministry that effectively reaches those far from Jesus and His Church with the end goal of "making Disciples."

Once understood, soteriology's relevance becomes profound. For example: If a ministry is based in a Theology that believes the evangelistic job is done when someone makes a *Day's-Decision*, their organizational philosophy of ministry will solely focus on that particular step in the overall process of *Evangelistic-Disciplemaking*. All methodologies based on this view can be described as *Counting-Converts*, rather than making disciples, and they will typically be designed around *Mega-Models*, rather than ongoing *Repetitive-Redemptive-Relational* Outreach Ministry.

Conversely, if a ministry is based on a Theology that believes evangelism is only complete when a *Dedicated-Disciple* is "made," their organizational philosophy of ministry will rejoice anytime an individual makes a profession of faith in Jesus, but will also incorporate missional activities that lead new believers into full spiritual maturity.

So soteriology is about taking seriously the Great Commission's mandate to "go and make Disciples;" which is more than *Counting-Conversions*! The vital importance of soteriology for SR&F Outreach Ministries has both Theological and pragmatic rationales.

A. Theological—The Biblical Way to "Go and "Make Disciples"

I'm sure that each and every SR&F Outreach Minister is of the belief that their evangelistic efforts are Biblical. I'm even more-sure that if the efforts of these ministers aren't totally Biblical, their motivations are pure and sincere. They truly desire to bring all within in their influence into a personal relationship with Jesus. Thus, none of what follows should be interpreted as being critical or condemning of a person or ministry, but rather, it is analytical and designed to enable and empower evermore *Strategically-Relevant* and *Efficiently-Effective, Methodological-Models* for "Going and Making Disciples."

1. The Main Thing: The Making of Disciples

If a SR&F Outreach Ministry is Theologically based on making *Dedicated-Disciples* it will rejoice each time someone prays to receive Jesus into their lives (*Days-Decision*), but will recognize this is just the first (albeit the most important) of many ongoing decisions and commitments that are crucial to long-term spiritual growth and formation (*Dedicated-Disciple*). As a result such ministries will have a plan in place to continue the work of the ongoing discipling of all new converts, with the end goal of developing life-long, maturing Disciples of Jesus. This plan would include engaging new believers in ongoing individual

Research Reflections

A 2017 Gallup Poll showed a decline in adult church attendance. Thirty eight percent of adults surveyed stated that they attended a religious service weekly. This number is down from 42% in the 2008 survey.
(https://news.gallup.com/opinion/polling-matters/242015/church-leaders-declining-religious-service-attendance.aspx)

— *Dr. Vickie Byler*

and corporate spiritual formation exercises and specific actions such as baptism. It also entails the new Disciples becoming a participating member of a local congregation. Ongoing and intentional mentoring and accountability are also essential.

Thus, the main soteriological question each SR&F Outreach Minister must answer is: am I seeking conversions, or am I, and my SR&F Outreach Ministry leaders, committed to ensuring all *Day's-Decision* (conversions) proceed on to the end goal of making of *Dedicated-Disciples*?

How this *Level #1 Theological-Truth* question is answered determines everything else a SR&F Outreach Ministry envisions, plans for, organizes, administrates and implements. This answer informs all *Level #2 Philosophical-Principles* that impact the overall organizational structure of a ministry, out of which all subsequent *Level #3 Methodological-Models* emerge. The obvious repercussions and results need no further explanation. However, beyond this primary rationale for establishing a solid soteriological foundation, there are a number of secondary reasons.

2. Evaluating the Effectiveness of The Sports Outreach Community's Soteriological Efforts

It comes down to simple math: Are we, *The Sports Outreach Community*, producing more *Dedicated-Disciples* today than we did yesterday? At least in America, indications are that there are fewer Christians each year, and attendance at congregational Lord's Day worship services is on the decline.

Thus, it makes logical sense that the claims made by *The Sports Outreach Community* have fallen short and the reports of conversions (*Day's Decisions*) have not translated into *Dedicated-Disciples*. The most that could be claimed is that the falling membership and attendance numbers would have been worse without Sports Outreach efforts. Undoubtedly, there is some truth to this last

Research Reflections

The Associate Director of Research at Pew Research Center Gregory Smith reports:
"Fewer adults are attending church, but not necessarily because they do not believe...Four in 10 say they practice their faith in other ways."
(Why Fewer Americans are attending Religious Services by Emily McFarlan Miller, Religious News Service, August 1, 2018).

— Dr. Vickie Byler
Lancaster Bible College

statement. I'm aware of enough anecdotal information to affirm there have been some who have not only converted but have also become participating members in local churches. Yet, I'm also aware of many SR&F Outreach Ministers who have shared their frustrations about not seeing the kind of Disciple-making success they desire. A majority of them are quite disappointed at the ineffectiveness of their current efforts. When further questioned they admit their efforts are primarily in producing sports activity, not Sports Outreach.

a. An Insidious Problem

One significant problem *The Sports Outreach Community* has is that there has never really been any quantitative or qualitative research done on the effectiveness of *The Sports Outreach Community*. What's perhaps even more distressing is it appears our community is afraid of what such research might reveal. A personal experience I related in a previous book in this series is but one example of this. In that "Time Out" I told the story about when I suggested doing such research on a particular Sports Outreach *Mega-Event* effort. The result? I was not included in future discussions.[1]

I ask you, my fellow Sports Outreach Ministers to warmly welcome, even intentionally seek out and support any such research. We have nothing to lose and much to gain. If the results reveal we're doing well, then we can rejoice and praise God. It not, then we will be able to identify what we need to do to adapt, change and revamp—all to the glory of Jesus and for the benefit of all who become *Dedicated-Disciples*!

3. The Bottom Line

At the end of the day, both specific ministries and *The Sports Outreach Community* in general, need to re-evaluate the current effectiveness of their

---

1   Putting The Church Back in the Game, p. 132

Evangelistic-Disciplemaking efforts. Each Sports Outreach Ministry, both local church SR&F Outreach Ministries and sports-related, para-ministries, are encouraged to engage in significant evaluations. The general question to be answered is simple: "Are we fulfilling the Great Commission?" More specifically, we need to ask: Are we really...

- **"Going"** to those who are far from Jesus and His Church ...
    - Or are we just welcoming those transferring in from other churches
- **"Making Disciples"** of the unconverted ...
    - Or are we just asking people to "raise a hand"
- **"Baptizing"** new Disciples ...
    - Or do we not care if they become baptized
- **"Teaching them to observe all I (Jesus) commanded ..."**
    - Or do we believe it doesn't matter how they think or act, just as long as they prayed a "sinner's prayer" one day

If not, why not? If not, can we honestly claim to be fulfilling the Great Commission?

B. Pragmatically – The *Efficiently-Effective* Way to: "Go and Make Disciples"

The reasons are not just Theological but also pragmatic. Good Theology leads to good pragmatics.

1. SR&F Outreach Ministry Job Security

Pragmatically, why is this of interest? If for no other reason the livelihoods of hundreds of local church SR&F Outreach Ministers and their sports-related, para-ministry brethren are being effected! Just a quick reminder, your job security is dependent on the effectiveness of your ministry.

III. Assessing the Current State of SR&F Effectiveness

Is local church SR&F Outreach Ministry on the upswing? Has it plateaued? Is it in decline? The most honest answer is it's probably all three. Again, more research is needed, but what we know anecdotally is there are churches that would identify in each of the three categories.

A. On the Upswing

Anecdotally we know there continues to be new churches that have seen the wisdom of embracing the *Philosophical-Principles* and *Methodological-Models* of local church SR&F Outreach Ministry. (See Timeout by Bob Schindler on page 22). This is also verified by the data that comes from research done at the REACHgathering. The research at REACHgathering reveals that two out of every three participants at the gathering had been hired within the previous five years. That's a lot of congregations that believe the SR&F model to be *Strategically-Relevant*. Whether it also becomes *Efficiently-Effective*, remains to be seen.

T I M E O U T

Local Church SR&F Outreach Ministry In Decline?
A Matter of Perspective!

"Sports Ministry in local churches is on the decline." I don't remember when I first heard this assertion, but it has certainly been a prevalent thought for at least the last ten years.

Proponents of this perspective point to the following:
* Churches getting out of SR&F Outreach Ministry
* Sports-related, para-ministries report an ongoing decline in the number of congregations using their services
* Denominations reducing or even eliminating their efforts to promote SR&F Outreach Ministry
* National efforts to support the sports ministry movement closing their "doors"

While these claims are real in some cases, they represent only one part of the larger picture. What these claims don't take into account is how many congregations have initiated SR&F Outreach Ministries in the last ten years. We can't say whether or not local church SR&F Outreach Ministries is in decline or growing until we compare the number of churches getting out versus those that are getting into SR&F.

The main problem in accurately determining decline or growth is: No such research exists....at least that I am aware of. Although the total number is in question, the following data provides helpful and hopeful insights. According to research in 2010:
* 36% of all churches have a sports and fitness initiative – either team sports, fitness activities or exercise classes
* That number increased to 40% for evangelical churches

This means, of the 350,000 churches in the USA, upwards of **126,000** of them are engaged in SR&F! In addition there are 80-100,000 evangelical congregations (a conservative estimate) and thus there are approximately **32,000** evangelical churches in America with a SRA&F Outreach Ministry!

While I recognize that this is just one data point and doesn't demonstrate any trend, it does communicate the immense scale of congregations involved in SR&F Outreach Ministry. When I got involved in the broader movement in 2003, it was reported there were <u>thousands of</u>

T I M E O U T

continued

Local Church SR&F Outreach Ministry In Decline?
A Matter of Perspective!

churches thought to be engaged in SR&F. Now we have real research that tells us that number is at least in the tens of thousands and may actually get to a hundred thousand. I was really astounded (and a little humbled) but also encouraged by this realization. If this is true, it means there are a myriad of American churches engaged in SR&F that aren't connected to the broader community.

My own personal experience validates this reality. I have the privilege of traveling in a number of different regions of America and I regularly run into churches who have been doing SR&F ministry for some time and yet have never has any contact with other churches, Sports Ministry organizations, or broader Church efforts.

I regularly find churches that are getting into SR&F ministry, not getting out. I also often find congregations that are building gyms/fitness facilities/fields to facilitate that ministry and are hiring staff to develop that ministry for the first time. So, yes while it is true that some churches are getting out of SR&F ministry, there remains a strong belief in the power and value of local church SR&F Outreach Ministry. It is even possible to imagine a net positive effect on the number of churches involved in SR&F Outreach Ministry if we consider the following:

• Society's growing interest in fitness in general and the corresponding growth and involvement in fitness ministry by churches over the last 10-15 years

• The developing work by churches among immigrants and refugees through SR&F Outreach Ministry

• The missional efforts of churches to send coaches, parents and players into community sports leagues

While there is a need for more specific research on this topic, I would ask the reader to expand your perspective and consider a very different possibility. With all that I have outlined in mind, I propose a very different picture of, the status of SR&F Outreach Ministry in the USA and I would ask you to look for signs of the encouraging trends that are all around us. Look around for congregations that are starting SR&F Outreach Ministry or that have already been doing it but have not con-

continued on page 24

T I M E O U T

continued

Local Church SR&F Outreach Ministry In Decline?
A Matter of Perspective!

nected with other churches or any of the national SR&F efforts. Find them and help them get connected.

Lastly, spread the good news about what you find. This different picture gives those of us invested in the local church SR&F reasons for real encouragement and hope for the future. This is the perspective I have adopted and hope you will too. SR&F Outreach Ministry in local churches is on the rise!!!

— *Bob Schindler*
Director Cede Partners

1. 36% of all churches in US having sports initiative - https://faithcommunitiestoday.org/wp-content/uploads/2019/01/2010FrequenciesV1.pdf - They explain the following - "The total N = 11,077 congregations representing a random national sample of congregations of all religious persuasions in the United States." The research page is here - https://faithcommunitiestoday.org/overall-findings-2010/ Faith Communities Today in the Faith Communities Today 2010 Frequencies for the entire population

2. 40% of evangelical churches in US have a sports initiative - https://faithcommunitiestoday.org/wp-content/uploads/2019/01/2010EvangelicalFrequenciesV1.pdfunder the same webpage as above - https://faithcommunitiestoday.org/overall-findings-2010/ - under the Frequencies for only Evangelical Protestant churches

3. For the 384,000 churches in the US - Christianity Today article - How Many Churches Does America Have? https://www.christianitytoday.com/news/2017/september/how-many-churches-in-america-us-nones-nondenominational.html

4. For the 138,240 churches in America involved in SR&F, I multiplied the 384,000 by 36% and this gives 138,240.

5. For the 32,000 evangelical churches involved in SR&F, I started with
   a. The Number of Evangelical Churches in America
   i. There are 45,000 in the NEA - https://www.nae.net/churches/
   i. This doesn't represent all Evangelical Churches. So have to come up with a better number
   iii. There are
      1. 47,000 Southern Baptist Churches in US - https://www.pewresearch.org/fact-tank/2019/06/07/7-facts-about-southern-baptists/
      2. 12,000 Assembly of God churches in the US - https://www.learnreligions.com/assemblies-of-god-denomination-700146
      3. 12,000 Church of God in Christ churches in the US - https://en.wikipedia.org/wiki/Church_of_God_in_Christ
   iv. This gets us to 71,000 - which didn't include: PCA, EFCA, Christian Churches, Evangelical Friends or non-denominational.
   v. Easy to see 80,000 evangelical churches
   vi. 40% of these have SR&F - this is the 32,000 evangelical churches with SR&F

B. Plateaued

Whereas it's fairly easy to assess and document new SR&F starts and new hires; and even easier to document former ministries that no longer exist; it's much more difficult to definitively determine if and when a ministry has plateaued. Two questions arise, even for those who maintain similar year-to-year numbers of participants.

First, what if the current year's numbers are within a few percentage points of the previous year? Can a year-to-year assessment actually tell if a ministry has plateaued? Perhaps a five-year benchmark could be a better reference to determine if it in fact has plateaued.

Second, plateauing also has an effectiveness relevancy. Even if numbers are trending up or down, perhaps the spiritual fervor has plateaued. So, while participant numbers are more easily assessed, spirituality is not quite so easily evaluated.

C. In Decline

Decline is probably the easiest to assess, and sadly, it is indeed happening in a number of places. There are a number of churches that have disbanded their SR&F Outreaches and many others have released the staff that oversaw these ministries. It's also easy to see when the participation numbers, activities offered and the numbers of new Disciples have dropped. This decline is of great concern to me.

Even if it can be determined that there are new congregations that add SR&F Outreach each year, this does not mean our *Community* is healthy, or even growing. Simply put, the health of *The Sports Outreach Community* is more defined and more accurately assessed by whether or not those congregations that have engaged in this philosophical-methodology continue to believe in its viability, than by the fact that new churches are initiating such outreaches. So, even if the total number is growing, the fact that many are abandoning their ministries communicates a most serious problem. However, I remain on record as saying many, if not all, of those ministries that are being eliminated due to their pragmatic ineffectiveness, are ineffective because *What* they do (*Level #3 Methodological Models*), is not based on Biblically-based, *Level #2 Philosophical-Principles* that have emerged out of solid *Level #1 Theological-Truths*…especially soteriology!

So just what is this soteriological flaw? That is the topic of the next chapter.

III. Soteriology or Bust

So, the real bottom line for both SR&F Outreach Ministers and local church leaders comes down to one thing: effectiveness. If the SR&F Outreach Ministry is built upon a weak and under-developed Theology of salvation, it most likely will not effectively "go and make Disciples;" and therefore will not fulfill its role to enhance and expand the church. In essence this lack of comprehending and applying a strong soteriology results in *The Sports Outreach Community* signing its own death warrant!

THE PRACTIONER'S PERSPECTIVE

The battle of **purpose** and **projections** often wage war in the mind of a SR&F minister...

The battle questions tend be between the **purpose** of answering the "Why?" and the **projections** that guide or decide the creation or continuation of the SR&F Outreach Ministry. As a SR&F Minister, I have found that having a clear understanding of Soteriology impacts both the **purpose** and the **projection** questions and helps me navigate through the days of upswings, plateaus, and declines.

When I begin to evaluate a new recreation or fitness format, a new league or a continued effort within leagues, I know I have to ask the developing questions from the **purpose** of Soteriology – How is it that the gift of salvation from the beginning, the present, and the future for all mankind is influencing and driving our programs and formats as well as our overall mission?

For me, it's not only understanding the **purpose** of our local church having a SR&F Outreach, but the understanding of **God's purpose** for the individuals that participated in the past, will join in the future, or are presently connected to our SR&F Outreach. The deeper dive into the individual(s) and the desire to see people not only make a *Day's- Decision*, but to also journey with them through SR&F activities towards *Becoming a Dedicated-Discipleship* is the model that serves our purpose. A model based on **purpose** encourages all participants in their faith journey and grows them and enables them in *Becoming* a reflective mirror of Christ on the field, in the gym, at the parks, and in the stands. Such a model is what creates the environment that stirs the soul to celebrate when the ministry is going

THE PRACTIONER'S PERSPECTIVE

well (upswings) or when the ministry is plodding through plateaus. A **purpose** model is even more important when we are wrestling with the harder questions that arise when we experience declines in our ministry. This helps me especially when I am faced with having to decide whether or not to continue or remove a specific methodological format due to declining.

In the midst of this we are often pressed and pushed by **projections**. **Projections** in themselves are not all bad. In fact, they help us with accountability and measurability within the ministry. However, when we find ourselves building off **projections** (making decisions to create or cut a specific program), we lose sight of the intended **purpose** (The Great Commission).

A deeper study of Soteriology for the SR&F Outreach solidifies our greater **purpose** in the universal SR&F culture to reach those far from Jesus and His Church (going); creates accountability of our ministries and programs concerning our main objective (making Disciples); and provides opportunity to see people redeemed, transformed and developed (baptizing and teaching).

— Greg English, Recreation Minister Cool Springs Church
& Adjunct Professor of Sports Ministry

Defining Soteriology in Relationship to SR&F Outreach Ministry

I. The Theology of Salvation—Why Does it Matter

II. The Theology of Salvation—Why It Matters to *The Sports Outreach Community*
  A. *Success-Statistics*
    1. False Indicators of Success
      a. The Prevalence of Authentic Conversions—
        Getting the *Success-Statistic* Numbers Right
      b. The Prevalence of Cheap Grace
        i. Cheap Grace: Jesus and the Rich Young Ruler
        ii. Cheap Grace: Easy Believism
        iii. Cheap Grace: Church Participation

III. Summary of Soteriology in Relationship to SR&F Outreach

I. The Theology of Salvation—Why Does It Matter

By way of a quick review, the word for the Theology of salvation is soteriology, and comes from two Greek words: *soter/soteria* (Savior/salvation) and *logos* (word or study). Thus, soteriology is a study of salvation. Why is this important for SR&F Outreach Ministers?

Christianity stands alone among world religions in its view that salvation is dependent upon and also a result of Christ's atonement. It has never been more important for the Church to be clear about the need for salvation, but also about the centrality of Jesus in that salvation. Let me be clear, concerning Christian Theology, there cannot be soteriology if there is not also a Christology! More to the point, soteriology is completely dependent upon Christology. Christology and soteriology are inseparably linked! The importance of maintaining, and how to persevere, in a Christo-centric perspective in an increasingly anti-Christian and multi-faith world is explored more fully in Chapter #9; whereas detailing the general basics of this vital concept is the focus of this chapter.

So why does any of this matter? What's so important about a Theological term that most people can't even pronounce, let alone know what it means? Simply put, SR&F Outreach Ministers will be hopelessly lost and confused about what they are to do each and every day unless they: a) know what their end goal is; and b) understand how to achieve that goal. Moreover, unless there is a resolute understanding of, and commitment to, Christ-centered soteriology, SR&F Outreach Ministers are susceptible to the prevailing multi-cultural, societal trends and shifts that will eventually bring influences that result in a loss of *The Trilogy of Gospel-Centricity*!

Let me make it even more clear. It is impossible for any person, any congregation, any Christian university or any denomination to call themselves "Evangelical" or believe they are engaged in a *Trilogy of Gospel-Centricity* ministry if they don't have a robust and well understood Christo-centric soteriology!

Thus, Christ-centered soteriology is an absolute must for all SR&F Outreach Ministers and Ministries, and therefore what follows is an exploration of how and why soteriology is relevant to The *Sports Outreach Community* in general, and will be followed in the next section with specific applications for the various specific expressions of SR&F Outreach Ministry.

II. The Theology of Salvation—Why it Matters To *The Sports Outreach Community*

In general, the most significant reason this is such an important issue is because there is an increasing skepticism about the effectiveness of Sports Outreach as a methodology and I believe much, if not all, of that skepticism is a result of an underdeveloped soteriology. I cannot state this too strongly! I believe this to be the single most important issue facing *The Sports Outreach Community* at the present time! Yes, there are many other pressing and vital issues, but I believe if soteriology was fully comprehended to the point of it empowering catalytic change, in how congregations reach those far from Jesus and His Church, we would experience a radical improvement in SR&F Outreach Ministry effectiveness.

My concern is expressed by many local church leaders and sports-related, para-ministry leaders who are beginning to question the current philosophies and methodologies used by the various ministries. At the very least these leaders raise the issue of stewardship as they question if the huge amount of resources that have been allocated to these ministries are really the most efficient use of their money, time, facility and effort.

T I M E O U T

Simple Church Re-envisioned

Author Eric Geiger joined me for the 2009 CSRM Sports Outreach Summit as a participant in the Academic Symposium part of the conference.

We discussed the principles of his book *Simple Church* in relationship to local church SR&F Outreach Ministry. Specifically he was asked why the book had included Recreation Ministry in a list of "activities" that congregations should eliminate.

After our discussion had shed light on how SR&F Outreach Ministry endeavors were indeed missional and not mere programs, Eric assured us that all future editions of the book would clarify the difference between sports leagues that were activity-based and those that were fully-mission oriented. In addition, he stated they would fully endorse the missional sports endeavors of any congregation.

Bottom line: When SR&F Outreach is founded on the solid *Ologies* (Ecclesiology; Soteriology; Missiology; etc.) presented in this AGON Institutes of Sports Outreach book series, it meets the Simple Church criteria in full.

This may have no clearer example than that of the recent "Simple Church," phenomena. Made popular by the book of that same name *Simple Church*, is now a prevailing philosophy in the organizational structure of a growing number of congregations and ministries. The premise of the simple church philosophy has great merit. I fully endorse the belief that congregations and para-ministries alike should remove any "program" that is nothing more than activity; in favor of implementing all that truly enables a fulfilling of a Great Commission vision and mission. Nonetheless, I believe the unfortunate result of the simple church philosophy has been the number of churches that have eliminated, or greatly curtailed truly missional SR&F Outreach endeavors. (See Time Out Sidebar on page 31—Simple Church Re-envisioned.) This loss of a most strategic way to reach those far from Christ and His Church is truly short-sighted and demonstrates a lack of comprehending how SR&F Outreach is truly missional— and this all stems from a less than robust soteriology.

Even with this said, I understand these kinds of things have been said, believed and acted on because so much of what masquerades as Sports Outreach is in actuality nothing more than sports activity—all the more reason for this book and this discussion. *The Sports Outreach Community* needs to sharpen its Theology of salvation so it can envision, plan for, organize, administrate and implement *Strategically-Relevant* and *Efficiently-Effective* Outreach Ministries.

A. Success-Statistics

Understanding what I've termed *Success-Statistics* is vital to attacking this issue head on. *Success-Statistics* describe the analytics that indicate whether or not a SR&F Outreach Ministry is authentically accomplishing its *Evangelistic-Disciplemaking* goals. In specific, it has two core components: a) Conversions (*Day's-Decision*); b) Spiritual Maturation (*Dedicated-Disciples*). *Success-Statistics* values both; recognizes both are necessary; and understands both are intrinsically connected. The first is not complete nor is it reality without the second, and the second cannot occur unless it is preceded by the first. The two together make up a complete and whole fulfillment of The Great Commission mandate.

The point of emphasis being made here is that most SR&F Outreach Ministries determine success by only tabulating conversions, not disciples. They do so to their own long-term detriment. Yes, the reports of large numbers of conversions are usually well received by church, ministry leaders and funders, however, these same people become greatly disillusioned when they realize that the number of conversions don't translate into other areas such as: baptisms, church membership, worship attendance numbers, Bible study participants and/or life style change. Be forewarned however...

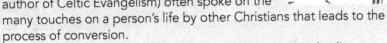

Research Reflections

George Hunter III. (Distinguished professor
Emeritus of Asbury Theological Seminary and
author of Celtic Evangelism) often spoke on the
many touches on a person's life by other Christians that leads to the
process of conversion.

He stated that "most of the people who became Methodist converts first joined a class and sometime later became a conscious
Christian". [1]

— Dr. Vickie Byler
Lancaster Bible College

1   The quote mentioned here comes form the book Team Evangelism Giving New
Meaning to Lay Evangelism by Larry Gilbert: Church Growth Institute Lynchburg, VA
1991. The quote appears on page 98 of the book with the citation on that page that this
quote of George G. Hunter, III came from an unpublished manuscript on John Wesley's
methods of evangelism.

1. False Indicators of *Success-Statistics*

Be forewarned; especially if you are serving a congregation that has previously
measured success in how many people have "raised a hand" to receive Jesus
each week. Your *Success-Statistics* number will probably go down. What this
means is, if your SR&F Outreach Ministry organizational structure changes from
seeking *Counting-Conversions (Day's-Decisions)*, to making Disciples (*Dedicated-
Disciples*), the total number of your initial *Success-Statistics* reports will go down;
both in the short- and long-term. This reduction in *Success-Statistic* numbers
is caused by two primary reasons: a) many of the reported conversions simply
weren't real or valid; and b) the prevalence of "cheap grace."

a. The Prevalence of Authentic Conversions - Getting the *Success-Statistic* Numbers Right

"Hold on," you say! "Why would we ever do anything that makes our *Success-
Statistics* numbers go down?" My response is not that we should ever do
anything to deter anyone becoming a Disciple of Jesus, but rather I am proposing
a better analytics system that may reflect the lower numbers represented by a
new way of assessing success. This is based on the reality that the prevalent way
Success-Statistics are assessed don't actually reflect reality and thus, aren't accurate
to begin with. Yes, they accurately portrayed how many people made a *Day's-
Decision* but the truth is that not all of those who "converted" became *Dedicated-
Disciples*! This of course gets to the very essence and premise of this entire book.
So the best way to describe this is to say while the total *Success-Statistics* numbers

may be lower, they will be more accurate in a Gospel-centered way. There is a second reason why the numbers will be lower, however.

b. The Prevalence of Cheap Grace

Reflecting over the past few decades, a brief overview illustrates how the move to make becoming a Christian appealing has "cheapened" the cost of following Jesus. Just to name a few:

The Lord's Day

- The Lord's Day has been reduced to a one-hour worship "experience," and is the now the norm for most of those who still make their way to a church
- Only a small percentage of "worshippers" stay for a Christian Education hour
- More young people play an organized sport on Sunday than attend a church
- Only a handful of churches still hold Sunday evening services

Marriage

- The divorce rate among Christians mirrors the general population
- Moving in together, once condemned as "shacking up," is now the norm

"Vices"

- Playing the lottery was condemned as the vice of gambling a generation ago
- Temperance is a completely unrecognized term by a millennial generation
- Whereas my grandmother lovingly warned me about going to the Cinema, today, those who call themselves Christians routinely watch movies that routinely use the Lord's name in vain and promote ethics, world views and values that are far from Biblical and Christ-honoring

Finance

- A very small number of Christians tithe
- Even fewer give sacrificially over and above the tithe
- Stewardship is another unknown term

Integrity

- Personal and corporate integrity are based on pragmatics, not Biblical mandates

Now I recognize the preceding "vice list" can possibly lead to some unBiblical "Puritanical" restrictions, but nonetheless, it should be apparent to anyone that cheap grace rules the day. What is communicated in most SR&F evangelistic proclamations of the Gospel is praying a prayer to receive Jesus as Savior or raising a hand to accept Christ at a church service makes a person a Christian and nothing else is needed!

Therefore, the second reason the *Success-Statistics* of your SR&F Outreach Ministry will be lower is because once the organizational approach is based on radical discipleship (which includes the significant lifestyle changes potential converts are committing to), it is likely there will be fewer *Day's-Decisions*.

Please do not misunderstand. I'm not saying there will be fewer real conversions, only the total number of conversions will be lower. This is because when the level of commitment is fully comprehended, only authentic conversions will occur. The following corroborative Gospel story demonstrates how Jesus approached a Rich Young Ruler and what He communicated conversion entailed.

i. Cheap Grace: Jesus and the Rich Young Ruler

This classic Gospel story demonstrates how Jesus called people and what that call to follow Him entailed. Even though the man called "The Rich Young Ruler" claimed to have followed all of the Bible's commands, yet he lacked a true willingness to forsake everything to follow Christ. Whereas, the rich young ruler's "idol" was money/wealth, what keeps people from following Jesus could be anything. The main point here does not have to do with what the specific "sin" or "idol" is that keeps people from following Jesus, but rather that following Jesus costs something.[1]

The relevancy of this and other passages for **The SR&F Outreach Community** has to do with what is communicated to those who are far from Jesus and His Church. Sports Ministries are less than honest unless they fully communicate what it costs to become a disciple of Jesus. Obviously, Jesus demanded the Rich Young Ruler sacrifice everything. Demanding anything less was poignantly described as "Cheap Grace," by Dietrich Bonhoeffer decades ago.

ii. Cheap Grace: Easy Believism

The admonitions about cheap grace as described by Dietrich Bonhoeffer have never been more relevant as they ring through the decades:

"Cheap grace is the deadly enemy of our Church. We are fighting today for costly grace... Grace without price; grace without cost! The essence of grace, we suppose, is that the account has been paid in advance; and, because it has been paid, everything can be had for nothing.

Such grace is *costly* because it calls us to follow, and it is *grace* because it calls us to follow *Jesus Christ*. It is costly because it costs a man his life, and it is grace because it gives a man the only true life. It is costly because it condemns sin and grace because it justifies the sinner."[2]

These profound thoughts describe a significant part of the dilemma we are specifically facing in local church SR&F Outreach Ministry, and even more so for the larger *Sports Outreach Community*.

---

1   Mark 10: 17027

2   Bonhoeffer, Dietrich. The Cost of Dicipleship. New York, NY: Macmillan, 1963.

SCOREBOARD

How Does Your *Evangelistic-Disciplemaking* Compare

...The Word is near you, in your mouth and in your heart (that is, the Word of faith we proclaim); because, if you confess with your mouth that Jesus is Lord and believe in your heart that God raised Him from the dead, you will be saved. For with the heart one believes and is justified, and with the mouth one confesses and is saved.
Romans 10.8-10

The Holy Spirit communicates through the pen of the Apostle Paul that salvation is both a head and a heart matter; that it is expressed in words, attitude and action. Is this reflective of your Sports Outreach Ministry?

When properly understood, the Gospel assumes that grace is costly. Of course, it dearly cost Jesus, and it also costs disciples of Jesus the ultimate control of their very lives. Any evangelistic efforts which neglects to communicate there is a cost to becoming a Disciple of Christ is not just "Cheap Grace," but is, in reality, dishonest and not truly the Gospel or grace at all.

"Getting saved" should never be reduced to a one-time, non-binding statement or a spur of the moment verbal confession only. (See Scoreboard How Does Your Evangelistic-Disciplemaking Compare, above) Rather, it is best understood as one step (albeit a most important step) in the spiritual journey of anyone who would claim to be a disciple of Christ. "Getting saved" assumes a life-long commitment to following Christ, regardless of what it might cost. This would include a willingness to forgo any and all athletic activities and endeavors and a commitment to regular and active participation in a local congregation.

Yes, our *Success-Statistics* will go down if we accurately describe coming to Jesus requires an "absolute surrender" to Him as not only Savior, but also Lord. That Lordship includes prohibitions against such things as drunkenness, abortion, cursing, sex outside of a heterosexual marriage, lying and stealing; and also includes proscriptions about such things as weekly church participation, tithing, loving our enemies, honoring the Lord's Day and our parents, and advocating for the poor, disenfranchised and oppressed.

So how are we doing? Can you honestly say your local church SR&F Outreach Ministry is truly committed to calling those who are far from Jesus and His Church to true discipleship? It's one thing to ask them to "like" Jesus on a particular day (*Day's-Decision*); it's something completely different to call them to truly follow Jesus as a *"Dedicated-Disciple"* for the rest of their lives!

Are we satisfied to report big *Success-Statistics* numbers to our congregations, even if they don't tell the entire story? My prayer is we will become committed to "go and make disciples," even if it means our *Success-Statistic* numbers are lower.

iii. Cheap Grace: Church Participation

The following questions must be asked: Can only one hour a week of spiritual activity really provide all that is necessary to develop *Dedicated-Disciples*? Can it really be said that churches that move from offering two sermons (one in the morning and one in the evening) and one Sunday school class each Lord's Day; to just one worship service each week, be seen as a truly effective philosophy for developing full spiritual maturity in its members? The spiritual depth of a disciple of Christ is greatly tied to participation in weekly Lord's Day services, both in the morning and evening, both in worship and in Christian Education activities, not to mention the necessity of participating in small groups that meet for accountability and fellowship! As local congregations give up the full Lord's Day, and individual disciples forgo the Lord's Day mandates, the spiritual vitality of the individuals and the impact of the congregation as a whole are greatly mitigated if not totally abandoned. I'm deeply concerned that congregations have indeed moved to expecting the bare minimum from their members and attenders.

III. Summary of Soteriology in Relationship to SR&F Outreach

So will The Sports Outreach Community settle for *Counting-Conversions* or *Laboring-Long* to "go and make disciples?" Will Sports Ministers authentically call those far from Jesus and His Church to not only confess with their mouths but to also believe in their heart and grow up to maturity? Will Recreation Ministers and Fitness Ministry Directors challenge all within their influence to "be measured of the stature of the fullness of Christ?"[3] Eternity for many hang in the balance!

Yes, what a SR&F Outreach Minister believes about the Theology of salvation is of the greatest significance. This of course leads to where "the rubber meets the road:" The core Theological foundations on which both sports-related, para-ministries and local church SR&F Outreach Ministries are based. It cannot be stated strongly enough that what is believed about soteriology is the most important and foundational aspect determining the *Success-Statistics* of *The Sports Outreach Community*. What is believed about this *Level #1 Theological-Truth* determines how a Sports Ministry envisions, plans for, organizes, administrates and conducts its outreach. Getting a Theology of salvation right, greatly ensures creating a *Strategically-Relevant* and *Efficiently-Effective* SR&F Outreach Ministry. This all becomes ever more clear in the following chapters.

---

3   Ephesians 4.13.

SCOREBOARD

Growing Up To Maturity

...until we all attain to the unity of the faith and of the knowledge of the Son of God, to mature manhood, to the measure of the stature of the fullness of Christ, so that we may no longer be children, tossed to and fro by the waves and carried about by every wind of doctrine, by human cunning, by craftiness in deceitful schemes....Rather...we are to grow up in every way into Him Who is the head, into Christ. Ephesians 4.13-16

Does this passage describe a *Day's-Decision* or a *Dedicated-Disciple*? Does this passage reflect your Sports Outreach *Evangelistic-Disciple-making* efforts?

Applications of Biblical Mandates of Soteriology in SR&F Outreach Ministry

I. Introduction

The vision and purpose of this book is not to provide a detailed, Biblical exegesis of soteriology. The reason for this is that soteriology has been explored in great detail over the last two millennia … by a vast array of the finest scholars and Theologians the Church has ever produced. I cannot hope to equal or better what has previously been provided. Therefore, anyone who is looking to fully understand the Theology of salvation, or desires to sharpen their comprehension of it, can choose from hundreds if not thousands of excellent resources that are available. Such Theological exploration and contemplation is greatly encouraged.

What I do feel confident in providing in this chapter however, are unique, relevant and pragmatic, proposals for envisioning the *Evangelistic-Disciplemaking* efforts of the intended audience of this book: *The SR&F Outreach Community.* To that end, this chapter will address and recommend specific applications for each of the following: a) Local church SR&F Outreach Ministry; b) sports-related, para-ministries; c) the staff of both of those ministries; and d) it will also include vital considerations for Sports Chaplains as well. What is addressed has to do with comprehending how to envision, plan for, administrate and engage in ministry that truly "makes Disciples."

Making *Dedicated-Disciples* stands in direct counterpoint to what so often happens in today's Sports Outreach. What takes place is what I describe as *Counting-Converts;* or put another way, settling for people to make a *Day's-Decision*, rather than encouraging them to become life-long *Dedicated-Disciples* of Jesus! To reiterate and more fully comprehend this, the reader has to understand that all too often *The SR&F Outreach Community* settles for getting people to "pray a salvation prayer," (thus, seeking a *Day's-Decision / Counting-Converts),* rather than putting in the hard work of going to "make disciples."[1] There is a significant difference.

Therefore the specific concepts within the broader spectrum of soteriology that are proposed in what follows are provided for the purpose of helping those engaged in Sports Outreach to focus on truly making disciples.

The first context is summarized in what I call: The *Trilogy of Gospel-Centricity.* The second is made clear in what I believe to be the absolute bedrock of ministry: *The Singular- Commitment-Cost* to *Evangelistic-Disciplemaking.* The *Trilogy of Gospel-Centricity* includes: 1) The centrality of Jesus; 2) The centrality of the Church; and 3) The centrality of the Great Commission. The journey begins with *The Trilogy of Gospel-Centricity.*

II. *The Trilogy of Gospel Centricity*

Gospel centricity has gained in popularity over the last decade or so; and

---

1   Did Jesus not say we should pray for laborers?! Making Disciples requires labor. Matthew 9.37f.

rightfully so. This popularity extends to both the commitment to ensuring the Gospel remains the focus and center piece of Christianity, and to the term itself. So what is written here is done so with a slight hesitation as it is not meant to either be a restating of this concept, nor an attempt to co-opt it. Conversely, *The Trilogy of Gospel Centricity* has been part of my thinking for at least 30 years and makes up the core of what I believe to be the essential foundation for ministry in general and SR&F Outreach Ministry in specific. Without this *Trilogy, The SR&F Outreach Community* is nothing more than a well-meaning secular organization that attempts to improve the earthly existence of those who participate in various leagues, activities or classes. *The Trilogy of Gospel-Centricity*: A) starts with Jesus; B) is understood and experienced through local congregations of The Church; and C) Has a laser focus on accomplishing the Great Commission. Let's start with what all of Christianity starts with: Jesus.

A. The Centrality of Jesus

Jesus is Christianity! Without Him, there is no Christianity. The difference is striking when other religious leaders and philosophers are examined. Mohammed was a prophet of the Islamic religion and taught people could be "saved" by observing the 5 pillars of Islam. Buddha taught many good philosophical things about suffering, pain and human attachments but didn't really talk about being "saved." Confucius offered much humanistic wisdom in his teachings, also with no real emphasis on being "saved." None of these men however, were God, or even claimed to be God. Furthermore, the religion of Islam and the philosophies of Buddhism and Confucianism could fully exist without Mohammed, Buddha or Confucius; but Christianity collapses without Jesus![2]

The striking differences continue: Mohammed said truth was revealed to him; Confucius taught about truth; Buddha said he knew the way to truth but only Jesus said He is truth! The profound distinctions become ever more clear when Jesus's own teachings are fully acknowledged.

Jesus clearly stated that He alone is "the way, the truth and the life." As if this isn't direct or clear enough, the very next statement He makes is drives home His point: "No one comes to the Father except through Me!"[3] Furthermore, in His

---

2   While only these three leaders of religious and philosophical communities are highlighted here, the same principles and critiques could be applied to any religious or philosophical group and leader. These comments are not meant to be totally inclusive of all religions, but rather, representative of how all pale when compared to Jesus and Christianity. Furthermore, the intent is not to personally attack or criticize either the leader or the followers of these religious groups. They are to be respected as it is assumed each of these were/are sincere in their belief and faithful in their adherence to the teachings fostered by each group. I will go one step further in commendation for such individuals and groups. I believe Christians share many common goals and ethics with the myriad of religious or philosophical groups and it would be wise to interact and collaborate whenever possible. However, as expressed throughout this book and book series, I firmly believe that Jesus claimed to be the only way to salvation and Christianity to be the only true religion (which this section of the book bears out) and thus all such interactions and collaborations need a Gospel-centric evaluation.

3   John 14.6.

conversation with a Jewish leader (Nicodemus), He stated that whoever believed in Him would have eternal life[4] and that God sent Him (Jesus) into the world to save the world.[5] To top it all off He is the only leader of a worldwide religion or philosophy Who claimed to be God.[6] This profound claim wasn't just stated by Jesus. It was further substantiated by the fact His claim was clearly understood by those who heard Him.[7]

Although these references to specific verses that succinctly articulate the claims of Jesus would be sufficient in themselves, it must be emphasized that the entirety of the Judeo-Christian scriptures affirm that salvation graciously comes through Jesus by His atoning work on the cross. Even more important is the fact that the united message of the entire Bible is that salvation comes only by and through Jesus; not through other people; not through other religions; not through other religious rituals; and not by philosophies!

Why is Jesus the only way? Perhaps the strongest argument rests in the fact that He alone was resurrected from the dead—not resuscitated to human life, but resurrected to eternal life! Comparatively, Buddha remains in his grave as does Mohammed[8] and while the teachings of Confucius have been unrivaled by any other human being and those teachings live on, he does not! He did not rise from the dead.[9]

The charge is often leveled at Christians that they are arrogant and narrow-minded in their claims that Jesus is the only way to heaven and eternal life. The charge is mislaid however! Christians aren't the ones making such a claim. We Christians only repeat and pass on the claim that Jesus Himself made!

The relevance of all of this for *The SR&F Outreach Community* is that Jesus is the reason Sports Outreach exists! While the improvement of a person's physical health, efforts to redeem sport and sports ethics and/or the enhancement of a family's relationships are wonderful by-products of SR&F activities; the major distinction and the most vital of all reasons for such Christo-centric endeavors has to do with connecting people with Jesus, not a philosophy or religion. Its laser focus must always be to connect people with Jesus—to have and experience a personal relationship with the Lord of the universe. Jesus is the only one who can transform the life of each person who becomes His disciple.

The centrality of Jesus is foundational and primary, but this is only fully understood and experienced in and through a local congregation of the

---

4   John 3.16.
5   John 3.17.
6   John 10.25-30.
7   John 5.18.
8   In fact Mohammed's followers honor his burial spot as a well-esteemed religious site.
9   I do not consider the teachings of Confucius to be on a par with the teachings of Jesus and the point made here is Confucius is unrivaled by any human being. The major distinction is that while Jesus was fully human, He was/ is also fully divine and thus He and His teachings were far superior to even such a great human mind as is found in Confucius.

worldwide Church—the second of the tri-partite *Trilogy of Gospel-Centricity*.

B. The Centrality of The Church

First things first. Without a definition of Church this discussion will be confusing at best and all specific SR&F Outreach Ministry will remain confused on how to envision, plan for, organize, administrate and engage in Great Commission endeavors that meet the *4-Fold Evaluative Rubric*.[10] By way of review, the entire previous book in this series addressed and discussed the definition, function and purpose of The Church.[11] Thus, only two ecclesiological points of review are needed to be made and explained here: 1) the Church is not a building; and 2) the Church is made up of followers of Jesus who gather together in local assemblies called congregations.

1. The Church: Is Not A Building

For the purposes of this discussion about soteriology whenever the word church is used it is not referencing a building. Rather church will be used to refer to the followers of Jesus who make up His Church with two specific designations. The first will reference the worldwide body of Christ and will be designated by capitalizing both words: The and Church. The second will be used to designate local gatherings of those followers and will be written in lower case letters using words such as: assembly or congregation. This is further explained by the next point.

2. The Church: Is Both a World-wide Body and a Local Assembly

Yes! The Church is certainly a universal body of believers; and yet that world-wide body consists of individual congregations and both consist of individual Christians. Yet, there remains a clear difference between how belonging to these two inter-linked but distinct groups is experienced. While each new believer automatically becomes a member of The Church upon a profession of faith in Christ; becoming a member of a local assembly occurs only when the new believer takes the necessary steps to become a participating member of a specific congregation. The reason this point is made is more fully understood by the following exploration of the interconnection of soteriology with ecclesiology (the topic of the previous book in this series).

The questions are: a) can a person be saved outside of The Church; and b) can an individual be saved outside of a congregation? The answer to both is yes, but that yes needs more consideration. Moreover, both the questions and the answers are relevant to SR&F Outreach Ministers in light of their call to fulfill the Great Commission mandate through a *Strategically-Relevant* and *Efficiently-*

---

10   See chapter 4 of my book, *The Fundamentals of Sports Outreach* which explains this more in detail. *The 4-Fold Evaluative Rubric* provides the foundation for ensuring each ministry remains consistently *Strategical-ly-Relevant* and *Efficiently-Effective*.
11   Linville, Greg. *Putting The Church Back In The Game: The Ecclesiology of Sports Outreach*. Canton, OH: Overwhelming Victory Press, 2019.

Effective, Evangelistic-Disciplemaking outreach ministry. So can a person be saved outside of The Church and/or outside of a congregation?

a. Can Salvation Occur Outside the Church?

Cyprian said: "Unless one has The Church for his mother he does not have God for his Father."[12] I believe Cyprian is absolutely correct, and yet if taken at face value such a saying can be misunderstood to the point of actually curtailing the very things desired by those who appeal to it!

Perhaps this is best understood by asking the question of what is to be done in a country or culture where there is no official, organized and recognized local congregation nor can even a single Christian be found. Can a person come to faith in Jesus in such a country and culture? Of course! God is not dependent upon people "spreading the Word!" He can, He has, and He will continue to bring people into a saving relationship with Himself in places where there is no visible congregation, no invisible Church, and no individual Christian. Furthermore, when that happens, that new believer is now The Church in that place and time! Yet The Church has not yet become a church (congregation), as that would require at least a second person who has become a Christian. It is firmly believed and hoped however, in fact it is expected that, that one believer would then inspire and reach others for Jesus and soon The Church births a church (congregation). "...where two or three are gathered."[13]

So, yes the salvation of individuals can occur outside The Church and thus it also can happen outside of a congregation. However, the normative way God has worked through the millennia is through local assemblies of The Church.

b. Can Salvation Occur Outside A Congregation?

Certainly the story of Saul being converted by Jesus Himself should be evidence enough that God does reach those who are far from His Church and any congregation; however, this is not the norm.[14]

However, the obvious answer is still yes! Salvation does at times occur outside of a congregation, but this is different than saying congregations are not necessary. Furthermore, it is certainly different than saying *Evangelistic-Disciplemaking* efforts outside of a congregation are the most strategic, relevant, efficient or effective. The Church can, and should, be planted by all means possible, but that's different than saying all methods are equally effective. I believe rooting *Evangelistic-Disciplemaking* in congregational-based outreach remains the most *Efficiently-Effective* method for "making disciples." Moreover,

---

12   *Corpus Christianorum*, vol. 3, pp. 5-7.
13   Matthew 18.20.
14   The specific reference to Paul's conversion is found in Acts 9, but the entire book of Acts gives evidence to the fact that the normative way God calls people to Himself is sometimes through the missional endeavors of an individual Christian (Acts 8.26-40), but most often through the activities of local assemblies of believers (congregations: Acts 2.42-27; Acts 11; etc.).

I believe the most *Strategically-Relevant* and *Efficiently-Effective* methodology available to congregations the world over is SR&F Outreach Ministry.

So, in summary, if Cyprian's wisdom is taken in a "wooden" way it could mean that unless *Evangelistic-Disciplemaking* efforts are organized under the auspices of a local congregation then all such efforts are unBiblical. This is much different however, than recognizing the vital strategic importance of rooting *Evangelistic-Disciplemaking* efforts in and through local congregations. That strategic difference cannot be denied.

c. Can This Make A Difference To The SR&F Outreach Community?

While it is true both the worldwide Church and its local congregations consist of individual followers of Jesus, the specific question that needs answered has to do with the exact nature of the Church's soteriological efforts. More specifically, the question has to do with whether *Evangelistic-Disciplemaking* is the result of the members of a local congregation who work synergistically to grow their specific assembly by reaching people in their community; or if such efforts are undertaken by one lone, missionary planting a church where The Church has no local assembly; both are The Church in action. This is a distinction with a significant difference as the following makes clear.

In one sense, it should be clear that anytime an individual follower of Jesus engages in Gospel efforts to reach a person who is far from Jesus it can be said The Church is fulfilling its soteriological Great Commission mandate. Such efforts would include all church-planting endeavors as well as any and all, one-on-one personal efforts to lead a friend, co-worker or family member to Jesus. Yet, while such individualistic activities are to be praised, the stark reality remains that these new converts are unlikely to progress in their faith and become *Dedicated-Disciples* unless they become intimately connected to a local congregation. It is there that: a) Biblical knowledge and Theological comprehension can increase; b) fellowship and accountability occur; and c) opportunities for service and witness abound; all of which are pre-requisites for overall spiritual growth.

This then, is the critical point being made here. The role and responsibility of local congregations for successful *Evangelistic-Disciplemaking* cannot be overstated. It is one thing to say it's The Church (the world-wide Body of Jesus) that brings a person to faith in Christ through both individual efforts of each and every Christian and by corporate, unified efforts, but it's a completely different thing to say the church (local assembly/congregation) is unimportant to the successful accomplishment of the Great Commission. My contention is The Church is most *Strategically-Relevant* and *Efficiently-Effective* when Great Commission endeavors are organized and implemented through local congregations.

Therefore, it follows that the most important difference it can make to *The SR&F Outreach Community* has to do with the vital importance of rooting all Great Commission activities and endeavors in and through a local congregation whenever possible.[15] All Christians are eventually and ultimately to be united with, and committed to, a local congregation. This then leads to the third part of the *Trilogy of Gospel-Centricity*.

C. The Centrality of The Great Commission

The full weight of the reality of what occurs every day is staggering for anyone who cares about eternity! Over 6,000 people die each hour! This means more than 150,000 die each day and over 55 million die each year! Even if we assume

---

15   I believe this includes the efforts of all para-ministries! Rather than operating independently, such para-ministries would be far more effective qualitatively, and experience far higher quantitative numbers, if they were to work within the parameters of a local congregation.

SCOREBOARD

What's Your Focus?

Are you...

1. Focused on Winning Games or Winning Souls

Has your Sports Ministry experienced a subtle, almost imperceptible, shift to winning the game; the league; the tournament; the state championship away from winning those who play on your team to Jesus?

2. Focused on Building Bodies or Building The Body

In your fitness, wellness or wholeness ministries, has the emphasis remained on reaching those far from Jesus and His Church or has it insidiously been undermined by emphasizing how to become more fit, well and healthy? Has your ministry changed from promoting holiness to healthiness?

3. Focused on Facilities or Families

In your activity-based ministries, have the efforts maintained the motivation to reach entire families for Jesus or construct and maintain impressive facilities for families to individually work out in?

4. Focused on Recreation or Regeneration

In recreation ministries, do the programs promote fun and fellowship at the expense of providing opportunities for establishing faith in Jesus?

half of the people who live in the world live in what could be considered a so called "Christian" country, that means some 3,000 people enter into a Godless eternity (hell) each hour! Is it any wonder then that the third part of the *Gospel-Centricity Trilogy* is focused on the importance the Great Commission being the guiding light for all SR&F Outreach Ministries?

At the very least, this should bring a sobering reality to all who believe a person's eternal salvation is totally dependent upon a personal relationship with Jesus. Yet, what does this specifically mean for Sports Ministers contemplating how to envision, plan for and conduct their ministries?

The real, over-arching question has to do with whether or not the focus of a ministry has succumbed to what is often known as mission creep. In essence, how mission creep impacts SR&F Outreach Ministers and Ministries is that objectives and activities other than accomplishing the Great Commission "creep" into positions of higher importance and thus the ministries fail to reach those far from Jesus and His Church. This slow "creep" away from the intended mission and focus (and onto lesser priorities) is most often unintended; but nonetheless real! Ministries that focus on biophysical needs and/or activity-concentrated endeavors are often more susceptible to mission creep than some others.

For example, in order for a Sports Ministry to function many so-called unspiritual activities need to occur. Fields have to be manicured and maintained; gyms floors have to be swept and refinished; locker rooms need to be cleaned and sanitized; and game strategies are ever present, pressing, and urgent. Fitness Ministry requires equipment to clean and maintain; classes to be prepared for; and new sound tracks and routines to be developed. Recreation Ministries need release-forms to be signed and collected; travel and accommodations to be secured; and publicity unveiled. All of the "pressing urgents" of SR&F Outreach Ministries can easily push any Great Commission priorities to a back burner. How does your SR&F Outreach Ministry stack up? The Scoreboard: "What's your focus?" (page 46) can help reveal whether or not the Great Commission remains central to your SR&F Outreach Ministry, or if your ministry has begun to "creep."

D. Summary of *The Trilogy of Gospel-Centricity*

So far we have focused on *The Trilogy of Gospel-Centricity* that can greatly aid congregations from experiencing mission creep. This included maintaining a laser focus on: Jesus; the Church/church; and the Great Commission. Next up is a discussion on *The Singular-Commitment-Cost*. Whereas the previous section on *The Trilogy of Gospel-Centricity* consisted mainly of my words; *The Singular-Commitment-Cost* is best expressed through a litany of Bible verses that will rock the world of any SR&F Outreach Minister who attempts to "soft-sell" the

Gospel or seeks to make it so attractive, that the cost of discipleship is neglected or watered down.

III. The *Singular-Commitment-Cost*

How many sermons can you actually remember? Most Christians will hear hundreds if not thousands of sermons and yet I've rarely come across any of my Christian brethren who can actually remember what the previous week's sermon was, let alone remember any of the hundreds they've heard since they became a follower of Jesus.

One sermon that has remained with me for nearly 40 years now was delivered by my dear friend the Reverend William Jackson.[16] What stays with me all these decades later is that not one of the words spoken in the entire sermon was actually my friend's own words! Rather, for nearly 30 minutes, Dr. Jackson only recited the words of Jesus. Even the opening line was from the Bible: "Then Jesus said…"[17] That sermon impacted me and remains an inspiration to this very day. I hope to honor Rev. Jackson by using that approach to communicate the need for *The SR&F Outreach Community* to rethink its soteriology.

So, what follows are not my words but rather the Words of the Bible itself. Collectively, the ensuing passages all make the same point: to become a disciple of Jesus is costly. This cost includes: a) to follow Jesus takes sacrifice; b) to believe in Jesus entails a faith that is active and often runs afoul of, and is persecuted by, those who oppose Jesus; c) faith in Jesus is not a faith of convenience; d) faith in Jesus is not simply an intellectual assent to a "higher power," but rather e) faith in Jesus often embodies suffering for the sake of loving and proclaiming Jesus.

The following Biblical passages should revolutionize the way *The Sports Outreach Community* envisions, organizes and carries out its *Evangelistic-Disciplemaking* outreaches. Let us be done with our attractional model of "easy believism" and begin to faithfully call those far from Jesus and His Church to "take up their cross and follow Him."[18] To that end, and in the spirit of Rev. Jackson, we begin with: Then Jesus (and the Bible) said:[19]

⁹"Then they will deliver you up to tribulation and put you to death, and you will be hated by all nations for My name's sake. ¹⁰ And then many will fall away and betray one another and hate one another. ¹¹ Many false prophets will arise and lead many astray. ¹² And because lawlessness will be increased, the love

---

16   Rev. Dr. William Jackson married my wife and I, and his dear wife Vail and children (Annie & Jimmie), have all played a significant part in my own spiritual growth and life in general. Their example of how to do family in the midst of a demanding ministry; the invaluable pre and post-wedding counsel; and their enduring friendship remain some of my life's greatest blessings.
17   Matthew 4.10.
18   Matthew 10.38.
19   The normal policy of footnoting each bible reference will be suspended for this section. In text citations will be used for both easy reference and easier reading.

of many will grow cold. [13] But the one who endures to the end will be saved." Matthew 24.9-13

[34] Calling the crowd to Him with His disciples, He said to them, "If anyone would come after Me, let him deny himself and take up his cross and follow me. [35] For whoever would save his life will lose it, but whoever loses his life for My sake and the gospel's will save it. [36] For what does it profit a man to gain the whole world and forfeit his soul? [37] For what can a man give in return for his soul?" Mark 8.34-37

[22] "Blessed are you when people hate you and when they exclude you and revile you and spurn your name as evil, on account of the Son of Man! [23] Rejoice in that day, and leap for joy, for behold, your reward is great in heaven; for so their fathers did to the prophets." [26] "Woe to you, when all people speak well of you, for so their fathers did to the false prophets. Luke 6. 22, 23, 26

[25] Now great crowds accompanied Him, and He turned and said to them, [26] "If anyone comes to Me and does not hate his own father and mother and wife and children and brothers and sisters, yes, and even his own life, he cannot be My disciple. [27] Whoever does not bear his own cross and come after Me cannot be My disciple. [28] For which of you, desiring to build a tower, does not first sit down and count the cost, whether he has enough to complete it?" Luke 14.25-28

[18] "If the world hates you, know that it has hated Me before it hated you. [19] If you were of the world, the world would love you as its own; but because you are not of the world, but I chose you out of the world, therefore the world hates you. [20] Remember the word that I said to you: 'A servant is not greater than his master.' If they persecuted Me, they will also persecute you. If they kept My word, they will also keep yours." John 15.18-20

[16] The Spirit himself bears witness with our spirit that we are children of God, [17] and if children, then heirs—heirs of God and fellow heirs with Christ, provided we suffer with Him in order that we may also be glorified with Him. [18] For I consider that the sufferings of this present time are not worth comparing with the glory that is to be revealed to us. Romans 8.16-18

[20] I have been crucified with Christ. It is no longer I who live, but Christ who lives in me. And the life I now live in the flesh I live by faith in the Son of God, Who loved me and gave Himself for me. Galatians 2.20

[11] Put on the whole armor of God, that you may be able to stand against the schemes of the devil. [12] For we do not wrestle against flesh and blood, but against the rulers, against the authorities, against the cosmic powers over this

present darkness, against the spiritual forces of evil in the heavenly places. Ephesians 6.11f

[29] For it has been granted to you that for the sake of Christ you should not only believe in Him but also suffer for His sake, [30] engaged in the same conflict that you saw I had and now hear that I still have. Philippians 1.29f

[5] This is evidence of the righteous judgment of God, that you may be considered worthy of the kingdom of God, for which you are also suffering. 2 Thessalonians 1.5

[3] Share in suffering as a good soldier of Christ Jesus. 2 Timothy 2.3

[12] Indeed, all who desire to live a godly life in Christ Jesus will be persecuted… 2 Timothy 3.12

[1] Therefore, since we are surrounded by so great a cloud of witnesses, let us also lay aside every weight, and sin which clings so closely, and let us run with endurance the race that is set before us, [2] looking to Jesus, the founder and perfecter of our faith, Who for the joy that was set before Him endured the cross, despising the shame, and is seated at the right hand of the throne of God. [3] Consider Him who endured from sinners such hostility against Himself, so that you may not grow weary or fainthearted. Hebrews 12.1-3

[12] So Jesus also suffered outside the gate in order to sanctify the people through his own blood. [13] Therefore let us go to Him outside the camp and bear the reproach He endured. Hebrews 13.12f

[13] Do not be surprised, brothers, that the world hates you. 1 John 3.13

[16] By this we know love, that He laid down His life for us, and we ought to lay down our lives for the brothers. 1 John 3.16

A. So What's a Sports Minister To Do Regarding The Singular-Commitment-Cost?

The answer to this question is simple and quick: make the presenting of the true cost of discipleship the centerpiece of all your SR&F *Evangelistic-Disciplemaking Methodological-Models*! Thus the simple answer is: Change!

Change the *What* you do, from focusing on *Counting-Conversions* and settling for *Day's-Decisions* to laboring to "make" *Dedicated-Disciples* by presenting the true cost of becoming a Christian.[20] Change entails both a "changing from" and a "changing to …"

---

20   All the italicized words found in this paragraph are either words that have been repurposed or coined to help define, delineate or designate concepts relevant to *The Sports Outreach Community*. The ultimate goal of this repurposing and coining is to create a common language that is shared by the entire *Community*. For definitions, clarifications and further explanations please refer to the Glossary found at the end of this book and/or read the previous books in this series.

1. Change From

Change from: "Begging" the middle-aged man playing in your "veterans" softball league to accept Jesus as Savior. **Change from**: "Selling" the parents of your youth league players on the benefits of the Christian faith. **Change from**: "Enticing" the person in your fitness ministry with all the health and body enhancement principles that can be realized by believing in Jesus.

2. Change To

Change to: "Discouraging" your 20-something, former Division I, Open League "Phenom," from praying a prayer to receive Jesus as Savior unless he is willing to make Jesus Lord of his life that would include moving out of the apartment he currently shares with his girlfriend and refraining from sex until they are married. **Change to**: "Communicating" to the family considering joining the church that they should only do so if they are willing to attend worship services each week, even if it means their children must forgo playing in weekend tournaments that occur on the Lord's Day and thus jeopardize a possible college athletic scholarship. **Change to**: "Informing" the Cross-Fit, competitive body-builder in your wellness programs that taking performance enhancing drugs is incompatible with being a disciple of Jesus.

In other words, the bottom line is this: **Change from** soft-selling the Gospel and **Change to** presenting the hard-core reality of discipleship. Before you can start asking those you are called to reach for Jesus to count the cost of becoming a disciple, ask yourself the question: Am I willing to count the cost of asking those far from Jesus and His Church to count the cost? If so, I believe your SR&F Outreach Ministry will be revolutionized and even if you see a few less *Day's-Decisions*, I believe you'll rejoice in over how many new disciples will be made!

IV. The Final Word – Soteriology for SR&F Outreach Ministry in Review

So in the final analysis, this book and chapter believes classic, orthodox soteriology has already been established by Godly men and women through the past two millennia. This includes the foundational message that salvation comes only through the redemptive work of Jesus. It is further believed that this Gospel message is best communicated and experienced through the Great Commission efforts of local congregations of the Universal Church.

In addition, this chapter calls all SR&F Outreach Ministries to present the authentic Gospel that stays true to the soteriology of The Church. This means that while the attractive aspects of being a disciple of Jesus should indeed be included; the Gospel should not be "sugar-coated." Along with talking about the blessings of following Jesus, the cost of discipleship should be a major part of all *Evangelistic-Disciplemaking* endeavors.

So the next step is up to you! Are you willing to engage in the hard work of evaluating your ministry? Are you willing to change from how you've always proclaimed the Gospel? Are you bold enough to embrace what my good friend Steve Conner outlines in his book *Rugged Discipleship* and no longer be satisfied with offering "cheap grace?"[21] Eternity for millions of people hangs on our collective decision.

May God truly bless and speed your efforts to go and make disciples.

---

21   Connor, Steve. *Rugged Discipleship* is to be published in early 2020 by CSRM's Overwhelming Victory Press (OVP).

Relevance of Soteriology to Local Church SR&F Outreach Ministry

I. Introduction – Who Cares About Soteriology?

Who Cares #1? While the families of most SR&F Outreach Ministers don't know or care about soteriology, they do care about their dad, mom or spouse keeping their Sports Ministry jobs … even if it's for less than spiritual reasons! (See "You've Got the Keys to…" Scoreboard below, pg 54). Regardless of why families may want such jobs to be maintained, keeping one's Sports Ministry job is a major reason for understanding soteriology because basing the ministry on a solid soteriology greatly enhances the possibility of achieving Great Commission success, and achieving Great Commission success ensures job security!

Who Cares #2? Billions of people would care about soteriology if they knew the eternal significance and horror of dying without entering into a personal relationship and having a saving knowledge of Jesus! This is, of course, the most important reason for understanding soteriology, for such a comprehension empowers Great Commission success, and such success impacts where billions of people will spend their eternity.

Who Cares #3? While soteriology is important to *The Sports Outreach Community* in general, it is perhaps even more pragmatically vital to those leading ministries and congregations. When understood through the lens of

SCOREBOARD

You've Got the Keys to...

Each year I would ask my children for their blessing and permission to continue as the Sports Minister of our church. The answer was always yes, but one time, my then ten-year old son paused before answering with a question of his own …

"Dad, why do you ask us this every year?"

I told him it was because I knew it was sometimes difficult being raised in the home of a Minister and that I wanted he and his sister to know they were my first call/ministry, and more importantly, I was willing to give up my role as Sports Minister if that was what was best for our family. His initial response was very affirming,

"Ah Dad, don't worry, everything's really good and you spend way more time with us than most of my friends' dads do."

His second response was more revealing…

"And besides if you weren't the Sports Minister, you wouldn't have the key to the gym anymore!"

Success-Statistics (a *Level #2 Philosophical-Principle)* these leader's ministries will be greatly enhanced. The individual models of *The Sports Outreach Community* consist of: A) Local congregations; B) sports-related, para-ministries; and C) Sports chaplaincies; each of which will be addressed in what follows.

II. Revisiting *Success-Statistics*

Before addressing the various models of Sports Outreach, it will be helpful to engage in a quick review of, and application of, the transferable concept of *Success-Statistics* that was introduced in Chapter #4. This review of *Success-Statistics* begins this chapter which explores how to ensure an authentic and accurate assessment of how well SR&F Outreach Ministries do in their Great Commission efforts. Then, each of the next three chapters will apply the transferable concept of *Success-Statistics* to the specific *Methodological-Models* of *The Sports Outreach Community.* Chapter 7 takes a look at sports-related, para-ministries; Chapter 8 explores the world of sports chaplaincies and Chapter 9 will then address the relevancy of the *Success-Statistics* concept within the context of an increasingly-secular, multi-cultural and multi-religious world.

A. False Indicators Ensure False Success in Local Church SR&F Outreach Ministry

Be forewarned, especially if you are serving a congregation or ministry that has previously measured success by how many people "raise a hand" to receive Jesus each week: your *Success-Statistics* number will more than likely go down. What this means is, if your SR&F Outreach Ministry *Level #2* organizational structure changes from *Counting-Conversions* (settling for *Day's-Decisions),* to laboring to "make" Disciples (*Dedicated-Disciples*), the total number of your initial *Success-Statistics* reports will go down, both in the short- and long-term. Chapter #4 gave the two-fold basic reason why this occurs: a) many of the *Day's-Decisions* (conversions) were not authentic; and b) the total number of people committing to becoming a *Dedicated-Disciple* of Jesus will go down if the "cheap grace" philosophy is replaced by a call to discipleship that "costs everything."

1. Getting the Authentic *Success-Statistics* Numbers Right

Hold on, you say. Why would you recommend anything that makes *Success-Statistics* numbers go down? My response is that I'm not wanting to do anything to make your numbers go down, but rather I'm stressing the need to get your numbers right. My contention is that your previous numbers weren't authentically accurate to begin with.

Yes, previous reports accurately portrayed how many people made a *Day's-Decision* but the truth is not all of those *Day's-Decision* conversions became *Dedicated-Disciples!* So the best way to explain this is to say while the total *Success-Statistics* numbers may be lower, they will more accurately tell the

Gospel-Centered truth about how many disciples have actually been "made." Regardless of whether it is because the re-envisioning changes the analytic number to reflect disciples, not "conversions," or because the new philosophy reflects the elimination of cheap grace, the numbers will undoubtedly be lower.

The vital question for local church SR&F Outreach Ministers is: Am I accurately reporting authentic disciple-making *Success-Statistics*? Having a Biblical view of true soteriology ensures accuracy that fully communicates true success.

B. True Soteriology Ensures True Success in Local Church SR&F Outreach Ministry

Soteriology is a major foundational pillar for any and all efforts within the local church *SR&F Outreach Community*. It is also foundational for re-envisioning the broader *Sports Outreach Community* organizational structure. Let me say it even more definitively. To be engaged in a local church SR&F Outreach Ministry without fully understanding, embracing and expediting a Theology of salvation is akin to attempting to have success in coaching a championship team without fully understanding, embracing and expediting a theory of competition and sport. It can be done, but at the very least, the team will be hampered in achieving athletic excellence.

SCOREBOARD

What can be done better?...

It's a simple question but its answer has eternal implications:
What can you do better on earth than in heaven?

Worship ---------------------------NO!
Pray --------------------------------NO!
Fellowship ------------------------NO!
Seek Social Justice ---------------NO!
Study the Bible ---------------------NO!
Love ---------------------------------NO!
Be Christ-like -----------------------NO!
Reach People For Jesus ----------YES!

So how does this change how you envision what you are investing your life in?

1. Getting the Organizational Structure Right

For example, if a particular congregation and/or denomination believes the end of their Great Commission efforts is to have participants in their sports leagues, recreation activities and fitness classes make a *Days-Decision* to pray a prayer to receive Christ, then the thrust of their endeavors go into creating opportunities for that to occur. Similarly if sports-related, para-ministries believe the goal is to have those who attend their sports camp or *Mega-Event* record their *Days-Decision* on a "commitment card," then they will organize their outreach to focus on a verbal *Platform-Proclamation* of the Gospel.

By contrast, if churches, ministries and denominations embrace a soteriology that sees having a person pray a prayer, raise a hand or fill out a commitment card to be the door—the first step—that initiates the *Becoming* of a *Dedicated-*

T I M E O U T

Our Job – Your Job????

Once, while serving as the Sports Pastor of a local church, I came to my office on a Monday morning to find my desk covered with "response cards." The cards had been delivered by a para-ministry using sport as an "evangelistic tool," and the cards had been filled out by hundreds of teens who had "prayed a prayer" to receive Christ.

These cards were filled out in response to a verbal *Platform-Proclamation* of the gospel given by a professional athlete at the para-ministry's weekend *Mega-Event.*" When I called the leader of the para-ministry to ask why he had deposited the cards on my desk, his response was: "our job is to get them saved and your job is to disciple them." And we tried to. In fact, we contacted each and every person who filled out a card.

Well, at least we attempted to, but we experienced our first frustration as it became obvious many of those teens had given bogus contact information. Even more disappointing was the fact not one of the kids we did make contact with ever came to our church. The motives of both the para-ministry and its staff were great, but their soteriology was underdeveloped, and their philosophy of *Evangelistic-Disciple-making* was found wanting. Only God knows if any of those who "checked the box to get saved" became disciples of Christ.

Disciple, their organizational philosophy will include subsequent actions and commitments such as baptism; church membership and attendance; financial contributions to the church; and becoming part of a Bible study or discipling group; and subsequently they will organize their Great Commission endeavors to empower that to occur. Sometimes, the confusion stems from belief that they are either called to evangelize or disciple.

a. Evangelism or Discipleship

The reality is, most churches and other groups within *The Sports Outreach Community* tend to tip towards one end of the spectrum or the other; choosing either to reach those far from Jesus (what is considered evangelism) or developing those in their church to reach full spiritual maturity (commonly called discipling). Churches and ministries stress one end of the continuum to the overall detriment of all involved. It is for this reason CSRM chooses to use the term *Evangelistic-Disciplemaking*. It does so for a number of reasons.

First, it emphasizes the importance of both outreach (evangelistic) and spiritual formation (disciple-making).

Evangelistic outreach is for the express purpose of making disciples of Christ and thus, the significance of the concept of *Evangelistic-Disciplemaking* becomes obvious. Both evangelism and disciplemaking are crucial and impossible without the other. The Church separates them to the detriment of all involved. Evangelism and discipleship should be considered as one seamless whole.

A congregation that only focuses on "deepening the faith" of their members (discipleship) not only shortchanges their members' spiritual growth by not molding them into "reproducing Christians," but also, will experience the eventual death of their church through the lack of any new people being reached and *Becoming* new believers in Christ. In contrast, and yet with a similar end, a congregation that only gets a person "saved" will not experience any growth because they are not producing disciples who become reproducing members who regularly participate in the body life of a local church.

Second, it eliminates the temptation to stop all *Evangelistic-Disciplemaking* efforts when a person recites the "sinner's prayer" and/or becomes baptized. When evangelism is the only focus, many churches and ministries fail in their responsibility to finish the job of "making disciples." The point is, evangelistic outreach cannot be separated from discipleship and vice versa.

As Martyn Lloyd-Jones insightfully articulates: "… a matter of believing on the Lord Jesus Christ, and we shall be saved … is one of the most subtle, dangerous heresies that can ever be offered … and yet it characterizes a great deal of modern evangelism."[1]

Thus, the descriptive phrase *Evangelistic-Disciplemaking* is more than just

---

1   Lloyd-Jones, *Darkness and Light,* 348.

some clever turn of words. When properly understood, it helps churches (and para-ministries) focus on the ultimate goal: "making disciples;" rather than solely emphasizing on one step in the disciple-making process: a *Day's-Decision* for Christ.

The *third* reason CSRM uses the *Evangelistic-Disciplemaking* terminology is because discipleship assumes membership and participation in a local church. It is a well-known fact that active and regular, weekly participation in a good church is a critical factor in the spiritual formation for individual believers and for the strengthening of marriages, families, communities and countries. "Getting saved" must assume a strong connection with a Christ-honoring, Bible-based church. As quoted previously, Cyprian wisely stated: "He can no longer have God as his Father who does not have The Church as his mother.[2] I join Cyprian, Calvin and many, many others in the contention that all Great Commission activity is to be rooted in and through a local congregation of The Church.

III. Obstacles to Success in Local Church SR&F Outreach Ministry

Setting aside the discussion about attractional vs. outreach models which will be a topic of another book in this series;[3] what follows will articulate a few of the obstacles congregations encounter. Each obstacle has the potential to greatly retard, restrict and render ineffective even well intentioned *Evangelistic-Disciplemaking* efforts.

A. Competition and Soteriology—The Negative Impact of Bad Competition on *Evangelistic-Disciplemaking* Endeavors

There's nothing worse than coming to the sad realization that the very tool that was envisioned to bring people to Christ and His Church—in reality—is doing just the opposite! Rather than serving to attract un-churched people, all too often, local church sports outreach creates such a negative experience that it repulses the very person the congregation is trying to reach! (see the Strike Three Time Out on page 60). This obstacle of the problem of competition surfaces in two main ways: 1. *Competition-Gone-Berserk*; and 2. *Competition-Gone-Soft*.[4]

1. *Competition-Gone-Berserk*

I once had to remove one of the most talented players in our congregation's open league. I had little choice in the matter due to the fact that he "jacked-up" an opposing player in the corner of the gym during an intense game. What made it really complicated was the offending man was not only a very good friend but more embarrassingly, he was also a pastor! When I asked why; his response was: "Because the guy continued to use the Lord's name in vain!" For some strange

---

2   *Corpus Christianorum*, vol. 3, pp. 5-7.
3   *The Mission of Sports Ministry: The Missiology of Sports Outreach* (forthcoming)
4   I discuss this issue of competition more fully in two previous books in this series: *Christmanship* (Chapters 2-4) and *Sports Outreach Fundamentals* (Chapter 2).

TIMEOUT

Strike Three and You're Out...

One of my very first experiences with a church involved being invited by a good friend to join a team his congregation sponsored in a local open league. Being athletically minded and competitive I welcomed the invitation. My enjoyment was short-lived.

The coach, while committed and well-intentioned, was over-bearing, egotistical and flat out anything but a winsome witness for Jesus and the church. While a number of the players were welcoming and accommodating, there was way too much emphasis on competition and little to no emphasis on anything spiritual.

Not only was that sporting experience one of the most frustrating of my life, I swore I would never attend that church.

Is your Sports Ministry attracting people to your church?

reason, mister "jacked up" declined the invitation to attend church.

It really doesn't matter what a congregation's soteriology is when competition goes berserk. When it goes berserk, the church has greatly lessened any chance it had to bring people into a saving knowledge of Jesus. However, this should not be interpreted to mean that competition is bad or evil, and should be eliminated from all church sports.[5] What should be understood is that when a Theology of competition is properly understood, implemented and enforced, it becomes the best model for bringing the highly skilled, trained and experienced athletes to Jesus!

This point cannot be overstated. It is imperative for every local church Sports Ministry to understand *Christmanship* and know how to incorporate it into its various leagues, tournaments and sporting endeavors. When competition is well-envisioned, wisely-incorporated and proactively-guided, it may well be the only style of outreach that has a chance of attracting hard-core, competitive athletes to Gospel-centered outreaches.

However, congregations often err more on the other side of this continuum.

---

5   This is discussed in detail in my book *Christmanship*.

2. Competition-Gone-Soft

Certainly overzealous, unsupervised and unBiblical competition has driven many away from church leagues and thus that congregation's chance to reach them with the Gospel was negatively impacted, if not entirely lost; but at least in these situations the leagues had attracted the athletes in the first place. More often, churches never have a chance to reach competitive athletes because church leagues have *Gone-Soft* when it comes to competition.

Going-Soft is the result of the host congregation sponsoring teams and leagues that downplay or even eliminate competition. This is done from a well-intentioned motivation and yet it is based on an uninformed and underdeveloped Theology of competition and sport. While more prevalent in youth leagues, the *Level #2 Philosophical-Principle* of *Competition-Gone-Soft* is also present in many adult leagues. This is typically manifested in specific forms of organized sports such as: "Low-impact" volleyball; certain forms of co-gender softball; and "slo-break" basketball leagues.[6]

To combat this, it is imperative Church Recreators and Sports Ministers establish a robust Theology of competition and sport for all they organize and administrate. This ensures Sports Outreaches that won't fail in one of two normal ways: a) jettison all competition; or b) take the attitude that "we need to accept and live with the unavoidable negatives of competitive sport." Both of these reactions fall far short of the opportunity to "redeem" the individuals within sport and the culture of sport, as both are the result of an underdeveloped Theology of competition and sport. Each is a sub-Christian approach in comprehending and dealing with competition and sport. What follows is a brief overview of how to deal with this obstacle that prohibits congregations from reaching those far from Jesus and His Church.

a. Jettison (Eliminate or Minimize) all Competition—This response is understandable and, in most cases, well-intentioned; but is found wanting on two counts: i) it doesn't recognize, nor does it communicate a proper Theology of competition and sport; ii) and thus, it sacrifices a most powerful opportunity to evangelistically make disciples. This *Level #2 Philosophical* approach of eliminating competition is ascribed to by both individual local church Sports Ministers and many para-ministries that provide sports leagues, camps and clinics for churches. It is based upon a *Level #1 Theological Truth* that mistakenly believes competition is evil or un-Christian. For these churches and para-ministries their *Level #3 Methodological Model* operates in such ways as to not

---

6   Mitigating and/or eliminating competition is certainly acceptable in specific situations and for specific reasons. It is wise to oversee the competition levels for children and there is wisdom in adapting the way some adult leagues function. Therefore, all slo-break basketball or low-impact volleyball leagues should not be eliminated. Such approaches are welcomed when such leagues are designed in such a way as to fulfill specifics goals of the league and meet the physiological, social or competitive needs of the participants. Rather, what is not acceptable is the elimination of competition out of a sincere but underdeveloped *Level #1 Theological-Truth* based on the erroneous belief that competition is intrinsically or inherently evil.

keep score, statistics or standings and often communicates striving for excellence (competition) or pursuing improvement (competing) are not Christian! Neither fit within orthodox Christian beliefs, nor are they what anyone really wants to communicate about Christ and Christianity.

b. Accept the "Unavoidable Negatives" of Competition and Sport—This response is less understandable but nonetheless a reality for many overworked and stressed-out Sports Pastors who are too busy to spend the necessary time to think this dilemma through. This *Level #2 Philosophical* approach is often the default perspective of an unknown, or perhaps under-developed, *Level #1 Theological-Truth* and it is the result of a lack of study and/or accessibility of Theological and philosophical training. Regardless, of why it exists, it should not be tolerated because it too forfeits a most strategic opportunity to make disciples of Christ by teaching all involved how to engage in sport and compete in the image of Christ (Christmanship). In addition, and perhaps even worse, the acceptance of negative behaviors within church-sponsored, sports-activities alienates the very people the church is attempting to reach for Christ! Most, if not all, people expect local church sports leagues to provide a high-level of organization and a most enjoyable experience. Yet when the "accept the unavoidable negatives" philosophy leads to the inevitable conflicts that surface, and these conflicts are not dealt with in redeeming ways, the alienated non-churched person leaves with a sour taste for all things related to church. Sadly, such churches lose a most relevant and strategic avenue for demonstrating to all who are not yet Christians the blessings associated with, and at times, the required sacrifices of being a disciple of Christ.

B. Lord's Day Issues and Soteriology

While this topic surprises most people as to how it could possibly be a problem, the second obstacle congregations often face has to do with how observing the Sabbath and celebrating the Lord's Day impacts their *Success-Statistics*.[7] In fact it's shocking to many Sports Ministers to know they are often the very ones who create this obstacle that interferes with "making disciples."

The first way Sports Ministers create this obstacle has to do with not just participating in sporting activity on a Sunday, but more-so, actually planning, organizing and administrating such activities; what I call an "anything goes," approach.

The second way they create this obstacle that adversely affects their *Success-Statistics* has to do with refraining from incorporating any and all sporting or recreational activity on the Lord's Day, what I call a "never on Sunday," approach.

---

7   I have written about the Lord's Day in relationship to Sports Outreach in some depth in the previous books in this series, and although I will not elaborate further on the Theological foundations for the doctrine of the Lord's Day, it is imperative for readers to acquaint themselves with the Theological foundations upon which its more pragmatic aspects are explored here. See chapter 6 in both the *Christmanship* book, as well as the *Putting the Church Back in the Game* book. See the bibliography of this book for additional books on this and related topics. Much of the Biblical foundation for this can be found in the following passages: Gen, 2.2; Exodus 20; Deuteronomy 5; Nehemiah. 8.1-8 & 10.28-39 & 13.15-21; Isaiah 56.2-6 & 58.13, 14; Ezekiel 20.1-31 & 46.1.

SCOREBOARD

Historical Significance of the Lord's Day

The Lord's Day came to prominence for the disciples and early church because of the two most significant events in all of history, both of which occurred on a Sunday—and by-the-way—both support the Sabbath principle in the fact they didn't occur on the Sabbath!

The Resurrection of Jesus (Easter)
The descent of the Holy Spirit (Pentecost)

The result? Two seismic shifts:

A Weekly (Not Yearly) Holy Day

Following in the Jewish tradition of designating "Holy Days" to have a yearly commemoration of significant historical works of God; these days were designated as, not yearly, but weekly "Holy Days." In comparison, not even Good Friday received this status!

A Change in the Sabbath Day

Perhaps even more incomprehensible and stunning, when considering the context of the Pharisaical movement in specific, and broader Jewish Theology in general, is the reality that the weekly Holy Day changed from Saturday to Sunday!

Thus, the historical significance of the Lord's Day indicates a profound argument for why all local church SR&F Outreach Ministers should sincerely contemplate what and how sporting activity should be engaged in on the Lord's Day.

1. Anything Goes

Sadly, many congregations have succumbed to the culture that increasingly embraces Sunday as a prime day to engage in sporting and recreational endeavors, often to the complete exclusion of any church related activities. It's more than watching an NFL game in the mid-afternoon or playing a family volleyball game in the backyard, however. All too often, local churches sponsor teams to play in leagues and tournaments, even when these games conflict with Lord's Day worship services, Christian education classes and/or youth group activities.

It's also sad that some of the sports-related, para-ministries have begun to host weekend tournaments, games and camps that take church youth and many of their family members away from Lord's Day congregational commitments.

While I commend the motivation of those who engage in these kinds of strategies in an effort to be relevant, and who sincerely believe such methods will effectively reach those far from Jesus, I believe they sincerely err.[8] The bottom line for congregations that have engaged in these endeavors is probably best expressed in the Time Out: "Once they've gone..." (See the Time Out on page 68). Buying into the false premise that creating evangelistic sporting activities that conflict with traditional congregational Lord's Day services based on the belief it will grow their church, ends up actually hurting their congregational numbers and impact!

2. Never on Sunday

Giving up the commitment to a Lord's Day goes hand-in-hand with spiritual malaise, ineptness and weakness. While the West has not yet seen what the French Revolution attempted when it proposed leaving what they considered the "illogical" and "religious" based 7-day week, for a more rational and secular 10-day week; for all intents and purposes, the ecclesiastical community has succumbed to the secularization of the Lord's Day into a day for family and the NFL.

Nonetheless, congregations that "throw the baby out with the bath water," and refuse to engage in any sporting or recreational activities on the Lord's Day forfeit a most *Strategically-Relevant* and *Efficiently-Effective, Methodological-Model!*[9] The summary of all of the scriptures found in the footnote #7, and also in The Church's doctrine concerning the Lord's Day can be boiled into three main principles. The way the day is to be honored and observed is to be as: a) a day of rest; b) a day of worship; and c) a day of witness.[10]

Therefore, does participating in and/or organizing sporting activities on Sunday meet the basic Sabbath/Lord's Day criteria? Does it provide for the tripartite mandate of rest, worship and witness? Can it be considered an act of mercy, necessity or ministry? The answer is mixed:

a. Day of Rest

Recreation can be part of the answer to meeting the mandate of rest but it should be obvious the refreshing renewal of recreational activities is much different than the tension and fatigue that often accompanies participating in

---

8   See my comments about the fallacy of such beliefs and efforts in my book *Putting The Church Back in the Game*, pages 70-74.

9   See my comments about how congregations can most effectively integrate sports and recreation into traditional Lord's Day worship and other activities in my book *Putting the Church Back in the Game*, pages 118-121.

10   Establishing Biblical Lord's Day Principles come from many different passages but Matthew 12 is as good a summary as any. Matthew is inspired by the Holy Spirit to record Jesus teaching the three Sabbath Day principles of rest, worship and witness through three clarifying "acts:" Acts of mercy, acts of necessity and acts of ministry. Jesus teaches that while the day is to be a day of rest, there are specific activities that would not dishonor the day but in fact enhance and fulfill the purpose of the day. To offer acts of mercy and necessity would be both a worship and a witness and would work in conjunction with acts of ministry.

professional or day-long sports.

Key Question: Does the activity increase and enhance the participant's health, rest and peace, or do they leave the participants exhausted and tense?

b. Day of Worship

Sporting endeavors can indeed be worship and sporting Christians cannot be condemned for worshipping God in and through their sport. However, as I've pointed out elsewhere, worshipping through sport is a supplement to traditional, congregational worship, not a replacement.[11]

Key Question: Does the activity promote and enhance the participant's ability to worship?

c. Day of Witness

The question of whether or not SR&F activities are actually missional at their core is hopefully never in doubt. If such endeavors are only activities however, then the whole purpose and premise of the ministry should be re-evaluated. Assuming they are missional, then by all means congregations are encouraged to move forward with Lord's Day sporting and recreational activities.[12]

Key Question: Is the Lord's Day sporting activity a significant aid, or more of a detriment to *Evangelistic-Disciplemaking*, including enhancing and expanding your local congregation?

3. Summary of Sabbath / Lord's Day Principles

Finally, Sunday Sport should be evaluated in regards to how it might aid and facilitate the *Evangelistic-Disciplemaking* endeavors of local congregations.

Sport on the Lord's Day should definitely occur if organizing, administrating and implementing sporting activity on a Sunday is part of a strategy that promotes a congregation's Great Commission goals. Open gyms or soccer "kick-arounds" following a Sunday evening worship service can be most relevant and effective strategies to attract, win and disciple those far from Christ. Recreational outreaches such as hikes, bike treks, picnics, sand-volleyball games, water skiing and many other sporting and recreational related activities can greatly enhance and expand a local congregation's Lord's Day activities.

So, what I am advocating for is to have local congregations envision how they can be both effectively and efficiently integrating SR&F Outreaches into their overall *Evangelistic-Disciplemaking* strategy. The key is they are to augment and support the overall strategy of the church rather than create obstacles to "go and make disciples."

However, there is a major difference between informal recreational sport/ activities, and formal professional/collegiate/scholastic sports.

---

11   *Christmanship*, pages 173-175.
12   For a unique model and perspective on how to integrate and incorporate SR&F Outreach Ministries with worship and witness see Chapter 9 in my book *Putting the Church Back in the Game*.

IV. Soteriology or Bust

Establishing the *Level #1 Theological-Truth* about soteriology (the Theology of salvation) is a primary requirement for successful SR&F Outreach Ministry and is a pre-requisite for setting in motion the development of a step-by-step disciplemaking process for a local church. (See Scoreboard – Salvation Success in chapter 7 on page 72)

Assuming that a congregation's soteriology is rooted in "making disciples," the SR&F Outreach Minister can then begin to envision how to organize around *Level #2 Philosophical-Principles* that empowers church members in their personal *Evangelistic-Disciplemaking* endeavors in the congregation's outreach ministries. So, rather than only planning one-time, *Platform-Proclamation, Mega-Event*-based programming, the organizational plan incorporates and integrates such endeavors with ongoing Gospel-centric, missional activities. This organizational plan is based on *Repetitive-Redemptive-Relational* activities and is designed to involve people over weeks, months and years, rather than an hour or two. The fruit of such an organizational plan will, in fact, only be fully recognized over the course of those years and decades because, let me state it once more: *Evangelistic-Disciplemaking* often takes years, not hours. A congregation that is expecting the completely secularized, non-churched, non-believer to become a fully mature disciple of Jesus in a matter of hours is being unrealistic and doesn't truly understand soteriology. Fortunately, local church SR&F Outreach Ministry provides the perfect and most effective, ongoing, long-term, tool known to the Church.

So, the bottom line for both SR&F Outreach Ministers and local church leaders comes down to one thing: effectiveness. If the SR&F Outreach Ministry is built upon a weak and underdeveloped soteriology (Theology of salvation), it most likely will not effectively make disciples; and therefore will not fulfill its role to enhance and expand the Church. In essence, this lack of comprehending and applying a strong soteriology results in a Sports Ministry that is signing its own death warrant! It truly is soteriology of Bust!

A. Why Soteriology Matters Revisited

Soteriology's relevance is profound. If a ministry Theologically believes their evangelistic job is done when someone fills out a card, prays a prayer or even gets baptized, their philosophy of ministry focuses only on that particular step in the overall process of *Evangelistic-Disciplemaking,* and the resultant methodologies will typically be *Mega-Events, Platform-Proclamations* and/or mass media blitzes. However, what successful *Success-Statistic* congregations believe and have found to be effective is based on a different approach and fleshes out why soteriology matters.

1. What *Success-Statistic* Congregations Believe and Have Found to be True

The congregations that prove to be most successful in going and making Disciples:

- Start with a Theological foundation that believes *Evangelistic-Disciplemaking* is a process, not a stand-alone event
- Believe the *Repetitive-Redemptive-Relational* philosophy of mobilizing, equipping and empowering church members to engage in long term relationships with friends, family members and associates is the most *Strategically-Relevant* and *Efficiently-Effective* tool The Church has to reach those far from Jesus and His Church
- Think these relationships are best established and enhanced in and through regular and repeated sports leagues, recreational activities and/or fitness/wellness activities
- Are committed to create environments that winsomely attract people into the church community where evangelistic conversations take place and relationships serve as conduits into the deeper walk with Christ and His Church
- Know all congregational growth is not the same
    Some congregational growth is largely due to what is called "transfer growth" (transferring one's membership from one to church to another) rather than "conversion growth" (joining a church upon converting to the faith)

B. Finally, Its a Lost and Found Problem

Is your congregation curtailing its outreach to the "lost," in favor of only serving the needs of the "found?" Such short-sightedness would never come into play if the congregation's Theology of salvation would have been more fully understood. Rather than going after what is called a "*Days-Decision,* the SR&F Outreach Ministry should have employed methodologies based on going to "make Disciples."

Choose you this day.

T I M E O U T

Once they've gone, they rarely return...

"This will just be for a season of time." That's what I often heard from parents whenever they made their way with their kids into the land of competitive sports. Now, don't get me wrong, competitive sports are great and Biblically defensible, but I believe there are huge ramifications to what happens as kids are allowed, and even encouraged to disengage from the local church for a "season of time."

Sadly, what I saw as a local church Recreation Minister was the inevitable result of what happened to these kids, and families. Over the course of a "season of time," kids are taught to replace the local church with devotions and prayers before games and listen to coaches rather than Sunday School teachers or youth ministers! Ultimately this "season of time" fades into a permanent, non-existent relationship with the local body of Christ. When families and children are taught to participate in sporting endeavors that conflict with church, the inevitable outcome is the "season of time" turns into an entire "lifetime." The kids rarely return to the church because they were taught sport was a higher priority.

I understand the hearts of all the well-meaning parents. They make these decisions in the hopes of a future athletic career of their young "all-star," or may even believe their child should honor God through sport (both are Biblically supportive), but quite frankly, statistics and Theology show a much different reality...

Just 2.9% of High School Seniors go on to play in the NCAA in Men's Basketball, and that just 1.3% of NCAA Seniors get drafted by the NBA! This means your High School senior has just a 0.03% chance of making it pro. Although I am not a betting person, those numbers do not line up with what I would call a wise financial decision. (These statistic comes from this source: www.ncaa.org/about/resources/research/estimated-probability-competing-professional-athletics)

On the flip side, did you know that by the time your young Christian is age 15, there is a 59% chance that they will disconnect from the local

T I M E O U T

church either permanently or for an extended period of time? Now I don't know about your philosophy for raising your kids and connecting them to the local church, but if there is already a 59% that they will be disconnected, the last thing I want to do is disconnect them for any additional "season of time." I suspect that even this 59% statistic would be greatly lower if parents wouldn't make sport a higher priority than church. (This statistic comes from two sources: www.christianpost.com/news/why-are-millennials-leaving-church-millennials-explain.html and barna.com/research/americans-divided-on-the-importance-of-church)

As a father of 4 kids, I too have a huge internal battle with navigating the church and sports dilemma. I currently struggle with these very things...how can I help my children find their way through this maze of church, competition, sport, life skills, and all that my children will encounter. One thing my wife and I are resolved on however, is we will continue to make participation in our church the priority.

Finally, if you're like me, we need some encouragement about God's concerns about our children. Ultimately this encouragement comes from knowing God is faithful and sovereign. Now that may seem like an overarching, "easy-out" statement; but it remains absolutely true. God is sovereign and God will accomplish His purposes for your children. Remember He loves them more than you do! As I've told many parents, "I do not know the future athletic plans God has for your kids, but I do know that He desires them to be actively engaged in the local body of Christ." If we as parents are to err in any way, I'd rather err in getting our kids over-connected and involved in the local church more than doing anything that might remove them from the fellowship of friends and believers that are going to hold them accountable to the things of God.

— *Chris Phillips, Lead Pastor, Journey Point Church*

Relevance of Soteriology to
Sports-Focused, Para-Ministries

I. Introduction – "Reasoning Together"

As stated in the Frontispiece entitled "Explanatory Notes For This Book," this and a few other chapters of this book are most difficult to write. The reason for this difficulty has to do with the fact that what I'm assessing and proposing may well make a number of good friends and ministry partners quite upset. So let me clearly, and as humbly as I can humanly state, what follows is not written to intentionally hurt or upset anyone; nor does it stem from a haughty spirit, suggesting that I am more righteous, Godly or intelligent than anyone else. Rather, as explained in the Frontispiece, it is offered in the spirit of "reasoning together" for the purpose of seeking truth in the hope we will all be better able to think; believe; do; and be; more Christlike. Here goes:

II. The Soteriology of Sports-Focused, Para-Ministries - Concerns and Questions

Again I'll say, this chapter may offend some of my dear brethren and ministry partners and thus, I start by sincerely offering my apology for any undue and unintentional offense that occurs.

SCOREBOARD

Salvation Success!

The following is a process for insuring a successful SR&F Outreach Ministry to "Go and Make Disciples"

- ✔ Train league directors, coaches, officials, class leaders etc. in how to lead people into a saving, personal relationship with Jesus (Day's-Decision)
- ✔ Prepare a step-by-step process for moving the recent convert to a disciple (Dedicated-Disciple)
    - ✔ Send the new convert home with a small packet that includes:
        - ✔ What they just experienced and committed to
        - ✔ What to do in the next days and weeks
        - ✔ What to expect during that time
    - ✔ Set a daily time to pray with them face-to-face or via the phone
    - ✔ Set a weekly time to study the Bible together
    - ✔ Enroll them in a "preparing for baptism class" and set a date for their baptism
    - ✔ Introduce them to and involve them in a small group Bible study
    - ✔ Enroll them in a church membership class
    - ✔ Set a date for them to publically become a member of the congregation

However, I risk such offense because I believe this discussion is needed so as to determine what is the most *Strategically-Relevant* and *Efficiently-Effective* model for truly making disciples of Jesus. It should also be stated that what follows is not focused on any single sports-oriented, para-ministry, or for that matter, only focused on the para-ministry world.[1] Therefore, if you think what is written has you and/or your church, ministry or mission in its sights—you may be right, but please know, other than one specific situation, it is written to a much wider audience and this critique can be applied across a very wide spectrum of *The Sports Outreach Community.*

Before going any further, it is important to communicate that I fully believe my fellow Sports Outreach brethren and ministry partners truly desire to "go and make disciples." Their motivations, heart and passions have never been in doubt; nor have been their commitments, efforts or ethics. What is in question is not the desire or character of anyone, but rather (what I consider to be) the ineffective *Level #3 Methodological-Models* they employ.

I further believe this ineffectiveness emerges out of questionable and suspect *Level #2 Philosophical*-Principles that are informed by the under-developed *Level #1 Theological-Truths* that they begin with. This becomes clear when the *Success-Statistics* of their ministry reports are analyzed.

A. Success-Statistics – What is Being Counted?[2]

Most ministry reports state how many people "got saved" through the evangelistic efforts of the various para-ministries—not the number of disciples that were made! Some of the more comprehensive reports include how many people were baptized or joined a particular congregation, but I have yet to see a church or para-ministry report on how many "disciples" were made! To state it another way, such reports always include the number of *"Day's-Decisions"* but rarely do they indicate how many *Dedicated-Disciples"* they "make."

Thus, the question that needs answered: is the Great Commission mandate about: a) "going" to get someone to pray a prayer of salvation; or b) to "go and make disciples...baptizing...and teaching them to observe all I (Jesus) have commanded?"

When these *Success-Statistics* are considered in the light of the Great Commission's mandate to "go and make disciples," it is easy to understand why this entire book is necessary; as it explores just what "getting saved" actually entails and means. Specifically, this chapter examines the question of what "getting saved" means to the para-ministry world.

B. The Theology of "Getting Saved"

So exactly what does it mean when supporters of a specific para-ministry receive a report that states "x" number of individuals got "saved" through that

---

1   In fact, I believe this critique is every bit as relevant to individual congregations and entire denominations.
2   For a deeper understanding of the concept of *Success*-Statistics, the reader is referred to Chapter 4.

TIMEOUT

"Getting Saved"

I once attended a Sports Ministry conference at which a number of "celebrity Christian athletes" were provided a "platform" to "proclaim" their faith. The common phrase they used to describe coming to faith in Christ was: "getting saved." Some told stories such as: "I got my assistant coach saved" or "he led me in a prayer to get "saved." What follower of Christ would not rejoice at these stories? However, as the late Paul Harvey used to say "the rest of the story" reveals many of those who had "gotten saved" never became disciples of Christ, experiencing lives of drug addiction, imprisonment and family breakups. These sad "rest of the story" tales indicated anything but a life of following Christ.

So The Sports Outreach Community must decide just what does "getting saved" mean and how is it relevant to their Evangelistic-Disciplemaking endeavors.

Perhaps more importantly, para-ministries need to re-evaluate putting high profile athletes and coaches on platforms to verbally proclaim a faith they haven't affirmed by years of living a consistent life of faith. The old saying is true: "don't talk it if you haven't walked it."

ministry's efforts? Does it mean these individuals prayed a "salvation" prayer? Got baptized? Joined a local church? Or does it refer to something entirely different? This reveals the real crux of the soteriological issue. I dare-say, when reporting "salvations," most if not all, of the para-ministries are referring to the number of individuals who recently made a profession of faith in Jesus on a particular day (*Day's-Decision*). Such reports usually do not include things such as baptisms, church membership or even any lifestyle change. So the real question remains: Is a *Day's-Decision* enough?[3]

1. A *Day's-Decision*—Is It Enough?

Salvation is often described and defined by the term *sola fide* (faith alone). This of course opens up the entire Theological debate that has simmered

---

3   I am not insinuating baptism or church membership is necessary for, or a pre-requisite, of salvation. I am careful to explain this throughout this chapter and book, and yet I believe the Biblical norm is for baptism and church membership to follow, accompany and in fact, empower true discipleship.

for millennia in the ecclesiastical divides between Orthodox, Catholic and Protestant traditions.[4] While I ascribe to the historic Protestant soteriological understanding that faith alone is required for salvation, all Christian traditions agree that faith alone does not equate to a faith that results in no change in the direction of one's life. So, yes, salvation is by faith alone, but it does not exist with a faith that stands alone. In other words, salvation by faith alone assumes that sincere faith is accompanied by, known through and evidenced by, a thoroughly repentant heart that immediately begins the new believer on a journey to an ever-deepening and constantly-growing relationship with Jesus. This relationship is made evident through the new convert's progression as a life-long *Dedicated-Disciple* of Christ.

Now, I've never met a para-ministry person who verbally disagrees with the mandate that they are called to "go and make disciples." Yet in practice, many of the sports-oriented, para-ministries that provide churches with sports leagues, camps or other resources fall short of the disciple-making, Great Commission directives and goals. They fall short in two specific ways: a) Theological; and b) methodological.

a. Theological—Easy Believism

The concept of easy believism (cheap grace) was explored in Chapter 4 and so only needs to be mentioned here by way of review. In essence para-ministries in their great desire to reach people far from Jesus are susceptible to the same soteriological pitfall of "watering down the Gospel" that is prevalent in contemporary denominations and congregations. They offer the "cheap grace" of a salvation that asks only for a *Day's*-Decision with no real explanation of the sacrifice or cost to those being called to faith in Jesus. The requirement of repentance, which means a complete turnaround and redirection of their life, is often not part of the invitation to accept Jesus as Savior.

b. Methodological—Easier Living

The end result of Theological easy-believism leads to a most profound pragmatic concern. Many vital pragmatic issues are neglected whenever the invitation to accept Jesus as Savior does not include making Him Lord of the life of the new believer. For example, it should be of great concern to offer a "salvation" that does not include subsequent evidences of faith such as: baptism; membership in a local church; participation in that congregation's Christian education offerings; Bible study (personal, couple, small group, corporate etc.); financial stewardship (including tithing); and personal outreach to others (witnessing)—just to list a few of the pragmatic changes that are associated with discipleship. So again, I ask the question to my dear brothers and sisters: Is a *Day's-Decision* enough?

---

4   This is another area where I state this book is not designed for an exhaustive examination of these Theological issues. Rather, it is designed to apply the Theological truths to the *Sports Outreach Community* for reflection and application. A search of the CSRM website and pod-cast archives is recommended for further study of these issues.

2. A *Day's-Decision* in the Sports-Related, Para-Ministry World

This section starts with a review of the current models of how the para-ministry world approaches soteriology and then proceeds on to discuss one specific model.

a. Overview of Current Para-Ministry Models

Each of the following are examples of the kind of *Level #3 Methodological-Model* missional outreach programs that various sports-focused, para-ministries offer to local church outreach programs. These models emerge from a *Level #2 Philosophical-Principal* organizational structure that has been informed by a *Level #1 Theological-Truth* Soteriology that is geared towards seeking *Day's-Decisions* rather than "making" *Dedicated-Disciples*.

• **Youth Leagues**—Perhaps the most prevalent resource provided to local church Sports Outreaches by a myriad of para-ministries is a youth league format that is organized for specific genders, ages and skill levels. Such leagues last approximately 6-10 weeks and usually include both a weekly practice and game. Participants take part in not only athletic but also spiritual activities each week. Typically, the culmination of the league's spiritual goals occurs at the end of the season in what can be described as a *Mega-Event* that includes a verbal *Platform-Proclamation* of the Gospel. This consists of a person of some notoriety (a sports celebrity or a person with a remarkable skill or testimony) and/or the Lead Pastor, Sports Pastor or another member of the church staff asking all in attendance (children, their families and friends) to profess faith in Christ via praying a "sinner's prayer;" raising a hand; kneeling at an altar; filling out a commitment card; or perhaps a combination of various options.

• **Youth Sports Camps**—Other popular resources provided to congregations by para-ministries are various kinds of sports camps that are typically one week in length yet intensive in the fact they are half or even full day affairs. These outreaches also end with an intentional call to accept Christ as Savior on the last day of the week, as described in the previous bulleted point.

• **Elite Sports for Youth**—There is an ever increasing trend in youth sports towards elitism.[5] Sometimes called by other names (Travel-Team; AAU; etc.), this trend now has a number of Christian-oriented, para-ministries engaging this world. The efforts of these para-ministries fall into one or more of three strategies: a) building of training/tournament facilities to host ongoing sports training, tournaments and/or sports festivals; b) sponsorship of tournaments, teams, clinics and/or sports training; c) production of curriculum for players, coaches and facilities involved in these endeavors.

---

5 Elite youth sport has exploded. I live within a three-hour drive of four sports complexes that are all designed to host elite sports tournaments, camps and clinics. Each of these complexes cost tens of millions of dollars to build and millions more to operate each year. These types of facilities are being built all over North America.

- Those that build such **facilities** do so for the purpose of hosting events with the hope of including some sort of Gospel presentation at the events or activities they sponsor.
- Those that sponsor **sports academies, events, teams and/or ongoing sports training** do so with the hope of being able to communicate the Gospel either through a *Mega-Event* and/or by creating *Evangelistic-Environments* for personal one-on-one *Repetitive-Redemptive-Relational,* opportunities for sharing the Gospel.
- Those that produce **spiritually-based-curriculum** for the teams that compete at these facilities do so for the purpose of providing the sponsors of such tournaments and youth sports complexes with Christian resources to offer the teams, players, coaches and families who frequent such activities and places.

To be fair, at least some of the strategies envisioned by these para-ministries are conceived with a "pre-conversion/ pre-evangelism" mentality and model of ministry. In other words, the belief is, that a large majority of those participating in this world of elite youth sport need to have Gospel seeds sown in their lives prior to them professing faith in Christ.

Nonetheless, these *Level #3 Methodological-Models* stem from an underdeveloped soteriology. The primary lack has to do with recognizing it's one thing to have someone pray a prayer to receive Christ as Savior; it's quite another to become a disciple of Jesus and commit to living a life dedicated to Him. More significantly, this model operates in the belief that being sponsored by or connected to a local church is unnecessary and superfluous, and results in the loss of a natural conduit to disciplemaking.

Not surprisingly, the sports-related, para-ministries that offer these programs, services, counsel and resources have documented literally hundreds of thousands (even millions!) of "conversions" (salvations) over the last decade or so. However, most of the sports-oriented, para-ministries that operate such *Level #3 Methodological-Models* are completely devoid of any connection to local congregations. Those who do connect with a congregation would be wise to broaden and deepen their *Success-Statistic* reports to include how many of those professing faith in Jesus receive baptism, engage in discipling activities and become members and participants of a congregation.[6]

---

6   In my opinion the sports-related, para-ministry that does the best job of empowering congregations to reach those far from Jesus is UW (Uncharted Waters). Each and every UW sports camp is connected to, sponsored by, and takes place in and through, a local congregation. This truly is the preferred *Level #3 Methodological-Model.* I would however, encourage my dear brethren (without doubt, some of my dearest brothers in the faith) of UW to go a step further in asking for the congregations they serve to record and report the data on how they follow up with all who profess Christ at these outreaches. I recognize such follow up is the congregation's responsibility, but the para-ministry can play a catalytic role by asking for follow up information over the following years. Such endeavors and statistics would be most revealing.

International Insights - Unintended Consequences!

In many countries around the world the sports culture can be similar to America, where sport has infiltrated many, if not all aspects of society. Fans religiously follow their teams as one sports season overlaps with the next. Professional athletes and coaches who are revered almost as "gods" are the most highly paid, receiving many times more income than other important jobs held by teachers, medical professionals, and builders. However, a main difference between the American sports culture and the rest of the world is how Christianity has infiltrated the sports world.

If you are a Christian and an athlete in the United States, often beginning in youth leagues, you were most likely exposed to a sports-related, para-ministry that in some why tried to teach how to relate your sporting skills/platform/experience to faith. This faith/sport connection grows as athletes compete on high school, university, and professional levels. Para-ministries have a strong presence and influence at each of these American levels; but it is quite different for Christian athletes in Europe and around the world. In those cultures faith and sport are kept separate. Not only are there generally few Christian athletes, but being a competitive Christian is a foreign concept. This is both a blessing and a curse.

The obvious blessing for American athletes is they are exposed to the Gospel. The curse in America is much less obvious at first glance. This curse while not always seen at first, becomes apparent over time and is brought about by the way these athletes are often discipled by para-ministries. By not rooting the disciplemaking efforts in a congregation the unintended result is that athletes become spiritual orphans because they substitute a para-ministry experience for "church." Another way the curse is manifested lies in the fact these athletes are rarely taught how to use their calling or gifting in sports to serve and become integrated into the Body of Christ through a local congregation.

By comparison, the blessing for non-American athletes who compete in a culture where there is a complete separation of faith

continued on page 79

International Insights - Unintended Consequences!
continued

and sport, is that they are never under the allusion that their faith is being truly nurtured.

Neither model is optimal, but rather a third model is recommended. Both situations can be greatly enhanced if The Church holistically embraces the SR&F strategy and vision and para-ministries embrace the local church. In this model, athletes can find a welcoming place (a synergistic collaboration of the para-ministry and a local congregation) to be: a) discipled and disciple; and b) be served and serve.

Sport is the language of the world today! There is no question about the fact that there are tremendous needs, but there are also tremendous opportunities in both America and throughout the world. The only question is: will the Church embrace the opportunities and engage in meeting the needs.

— *P. F. Myers, CSRM International Director*

So once again, the question must be asked: how valid are the reported *Success-Statistics* if the individuals who make a *Day's-Decision* never connect with a congregation or become mature, growing Christians (*Dedicated-Disciples*)? This in and of itself demonstrates that a *Day's-Decision* is not enough.

b. One Specific Para-Ministry Model

There's no way to maintain the anonymity of the specific para-ministry that will be discussed at this point, and thus it would be fruitless to even try. Nonetheless my motivation remains the same. My comments are an attempt to begin to "reason together." They are not criticism (attacking the people or ministry) but rather critique (addressing the issue). My hope is that this discussion will promote a pro-active conversation that will lead to our entire *Community* being able to discover the most *Strategically-Relevant* and *Efficiently-Effective Evangelistic-Disciplemaking* models we've ever experienced.

As to the one para-ministry model…

One specific aspect of the soteriology espoused by Cru (formerly Campus Crusade for Christ) is questionable and will be critiqued and a second will be more severely assessed and addressed. However, these critiques are not holistic condemnations of a most wonderful para-ministry.[7]

Cru's commitment to evangelism is exemplary! Yet I have concerns about Cru's (and its Sports Ministry wing Athletes in Action—AIA) approach to evangelism. I believe their approach to evangelism is underdeveloped in one area (having to do with the *Day's-Decision/Dedicated-Disciples* concept); and I believe it is actually heretical in another (the carnal Christian concept). This errant Theology results in how they envision, organize and operate their ministry.[8]

Now before I'm burned at the stake, let me quickly state two things. First, I was greatly impacted in a most positive way by the ministry of Cru. I attended Explo 72 and in addition, was personally discipled by Dr. James Miller in basic Christianity through CCC's courses.[9] Secondly, I continue to personally support AIA and Cru staff because I believe in them and want to support their efforts to reach those far from Jesus and His Church. Nonetheless, I remain greatly troubled by Cru's soteriology, and more so, by the end result of what it leads to.

The basic Theology of salvation (soteriology) for Cru can be summed up as: leading someone to pray a prayer in which the "unsaved" person invites Jesus to come into their life, thus accepting Jesus Christ as their Savior. I believe Cru's/AIA's motivations are appropriate and to be applauded, and I fully support these efforts and goals up to and through this point. I support it because such prayers are the logical and necessary first steps for beginning a life as a disciple of Christ. Thus these prayers and actions are of the utmost value.[10] However, what ensues after the initial prayer is where Cru's basic Theology of salvation is of concern, and this concern continues where it directly impacts the methodology of AIA.

The simple question being raised is: is praying a prayer for salvation enough?

---

7 My personal policy and the policy of Overwhelming Victory Press are generally to refer by name to individual ministries or ministers only when such comments are supportive, exemplary and complementary (see the previous footnote that affirms UW). Furthermore the personal and corporate policy is to avoid mentioning the name of the ministry, mission or person if they are being critiqued in what may be seen as a negative light. However, there is no way to hide behind anonymity in this case. Cru/AIA have clearly made the concept of the carnal Christian a foundational piece of their thinking and staff training. Therefore, in this case, an exception is made and this wonderful and well-intentioned mission is specifically mentioned. It should not be misconstrued however, that any ill will is intended or that we've slipped into criticism (attacking people), but rather these comments are offered as critique (addressing the issue) in the spirit of "reasoning together" and in hope of future reconciliation of the Theological differences. The intent here is to be analytical, not critical; all with the end goal of aiding *The Sports Outreach Community* to achieve its Great Commission goals.

8 By heretical I do not mean apostate. To be apostate means to have completely denied the truth of the entirety of Christian Theology and be completely turned away from Christ, whereas heretical refers to having an errant Theological belief in one specific tenet of Theology. I believe the concept of the carnal Christian to be heretical but Cru and AIA are still faithful in their pursuit of Jesus.

9 I will be eternally grateful to Dr. Miller. Not only did he sponsor me to go to Explo 72 but he also took on the mammoth task of discipling such an untested novice and renegade like me. He remains one of my personal heroes in the faith. My life was forever impacted by his faithful obedience to Jesus. He saw in me a potential, I didn't know was there and I've been forever grateful for his sacrificial impact on my life.

10 By "such prayers" I do not assume that Cru's suggested "sinner's prayer" is the "magic bullet" but rather only one example of the kind of prayer that is needed to initiate a personal relationship with Jesus. The specifically worded prayers found in the tracts of Campus Crusade serve as a good model as it represents a contrite and truly repentant heart. The order in which such words occur or what specific words are used matters less than the heart and mind that utters the words.

International Insights
Competing or Cooperating

A sports-related, para-ministry in the U. K. stopped promoting the development of church sports ministries because they feared by doing so they would encourage coaches and athletes to leave their secular teams (the world) to join church teams (their Christian Family).

The para-ministry highly valued the opportunity Christian athletes had to be examples for Jesus to unbelievers on their secular teams. They further reasoned the athletes would most often only minister to other Christians on the church teams. Thus, by calling Christian athletes out of the secular athletic world a most strategic platform for sharing the Gospel would be lost.

A subsequent tug-of-war was created because most of the churches had indeed become ingrown and were not reaching out effectively, and yet even if a non-believing player from a secular team professed faith in Jesus through the ministry of a Christian teammate, could the new believer be truly discipled without connecting them to a local congregation?

It is my opinion embracing a strategy that combines both "playing in the world" and "playing in the church" can be effective when a congregation and a para-ministry partner together and mutually discover how to become relevant in its own secular sports community AND trains its sports people to: a) have a heart that is actively and intentionally ministering to the world; and b) knows how to connect those far from Jesus to a local church body.

— *P. F. Myers, CSRM International Director*

This soteriological foundation leads to another troubling concern—Cru's concept of the "carnal Christian."[11]

i. Is The Carnal Christian Concept Helpful?

Whereas, the previous discussion about Cru's perspective of a *Day's-Decision* is cause for concern, I believe the concept of being a "carnal Christian" is: a) Theologically heretical; b) logically fallacious; and c) pragmatically problematic because it promulgates one of the most troubling teachings about a person's salvation currently expressed in the *Sports Outreach Community*. To repeat, but to say it another way, I am disturbed by what is meant and communicated by the phrase: "carnal Christian" because I believe it is unBiblical and thus can be devastating to the spiritual life of individuals, their relationship with Jesus and their discipleship progression.

The teaching about being a carnal Christian is best understood through Cru's graphics and literature. The graphics in these materials include a circle that encompasses a "throne," a cross and a letter "S" within. The circle represents a person's life. The throne represents what controls or heads one's life. The cross represents Jesus and the "S" is used to communicate the person in question. All three symbols are placed in the circle. So, the circle represents the life of a person and whatever sits upon the throne of that life is what dominates and controls that life. If the cross sits on the throne and the "S" sits at the foot of the throne, then this life is understood to be one where Christ is not only the Savior but also Lord. However, if the "S" sits on the throne and the cross rests at the foot of it, this graphically communicates the individual person retains "lordship," but because Jesus is still in the person's life this person would still be considered a Christian but alas a "carnal Christian." For Cru/AIA staff, either scenario would be deemed success, albeit the cross on the throne version is preferred.

ii. Connecting the Soteriology of the "Carnal Christian" Concept and AIA's Methodology

To be fair, I have never met a Cru/AIA staff person who said the carnal Christian status is the goal of their ministry, and most work diligently to have the people they are reaching out to, get the "S" off and the cross on the throne of their life. However, this carnal Christian *Level #1 Theological Truth* doctrine has unfortunately led to troubling *Level #3 Methodological Models*.

Even though I am troubled by the carnal Christian Theology, I understand the motivation behind Cru's thinking; and in a certain framework, it has merit. The merit is in trying to relieve the concern of followers of Jesus who are worried when they fall short of living a fully sanctified life. The goals of communicating the concept of carnal Christians are to be commended when done so as to

---

11   The term "carnal" in the phrase "carnal Christian" is derived from the same word as carnivorous and incarnational—as in incarnational evangelism. Carnal has to do with the flesh and when it is used by Cru it is done so as to describe a person who allows "fleshly" desires to consistently and constantly be the lord of their life, rather than allowing Jesus to be the Lord of their life.

reassure new or immature believers they are still Christians even if they aren't perfect; or to communicate to disciples of Jesus to not be unduly concerned when they periodically come to a realization of another area of life they have not fully relinquished to Jesus. However, this is quite different than teaching a person is truly a Christian if they are unwilling to put Jesus on, and keep Him on, "the throne" of their life.[12]

What is subtly communicated by the carnal Christian teaching is all that is necessary to receive eternal life and to consider oneself a Christian is: Pray a prayer that gets Jesus in their life, even if they never intend to put Him on the throne of their life as Lord. This is the epitome of Bonhoeffer's "easy believism," to escape the eternal damnation of hell but still be able to "Go your own merry way." I believe this has negatively impacted Christianity in general and *The Sports Outreach Community* specifically in how it has become one of the greatest influences in shaping the *Level #2 Philosophical-Principles* organizational structures of many within *The Sports Outreach Community.*

This is not to say, that new believers don't act "in the flesh" on occasion, but rather that, while at times falling into fleshly sin, Jesus remains not only Savior but most importantly, the ultimate Lord of one's life.

In summary then, AIA truly believes: a) all an athlete or coach need do is pray a "sinners" prayer; and b) never truly repent (turn away from) their "fleshly/carnal" ways and; c) never attempt to live a Christ-honoring life; d) never become baptized; and e) never join and become active in a local congregation. This belief then leads to their *Level #2 Philosophical-Principles* organizational approach to ministry which subsequently results in their *Level #3 Methodological-Model* outreach ministry end goal of seeking to have athletes and coaches pray such a prayer; then requiring nothing more. Such methodology is made evident by the Gospel tracts they have produced; how their outreach is structured; and the *Success-Statistic* reports they provide to financial supporters.[13]

However, if AIA believes they are commissioned to "go and make disciples" (including baptism, participation in a local congregation, holiness etc.), their ministry will be envisioned and conducted much differently. Not the least of which would be to anchor each and every AIA ministry in and through a local congregation!

3. A Day's-Decision—In The Christian Camp World

Another related para-ministry methodology is camping. This includes both day-camps and overnight, residential camps. Most day-camps are administrated

---

12   In this concept of being a carnal Christian, what is taught is a person is truly and fully a Christian; will spend eternity in heaven with Jesus; and can claim they are worthy of all benefits afforded to Christians; despite the fact that Jesus is not sitting on the throne of their life; meaning He is not Lord of their life.

13   Again, my experience has revealed that individual AIA and Cru staff members are quick to state discipleship is important. Yet their *Success-Statistics* only report how many *Day's-Decisions* are received, not how many *Dedicated-Disciples* are made with the requisite of long term membership in a local congregation etc.

by and held at the site of a congregation whereas most residential camps are typically held in more rustic environments and would be considered more of a para-ministry than a local church ministry. It is to the independent residential camps that this brief section is addressed.

It is generally accepted that many people indicate they first experienced Christ; initiated their faith in Christ; and/or their faith was greatly impacted at and through a Christian camp. Yet, many of those who indicated they had some "religious experience or awakening" at a camp report that initial fervor faded over the ensuing weeks and months that followed.[14]

I believe this is yet another reason to link all camps to a specific congregation. It's one thing to "send kids to a Christian camp;" it's quite another for the youth pastors, youth advisors and other congregational members to take kids to a camp. These leaders can then seamlessly continue disciplemaking through the church that sponsors and runs the camp.

Thus, a very similar question remains for all independent camp directors: "Is a *Day's-Decision* enough?" The evidence would seem to indicate the likelihood of the making of *Dedicated-Disciples* is greatly enhanced when campers who profess faith in Christ at camp are immediately connected with a nurturing local church.

III. Summary Of The Relevance of Soteriology for Sports-Related, Para-Ministries

In an effort to make the Gospel winsome and attractive, the para-ministry world's evangelism efforts often communicate the bare minimum of what is needed to become a Christian, not the full explanation of what it means to become a disciple. It appears The Church as manifested through many para-ministries strives not for disciples but for decisions. They prefer to engage in *Counting-Conversions* rather than going to make *Dedicated-Disciples*.

To that end the following questions must be answered:
- Are the current para-ministry *Level #3 Methodological-Models* effective at successfully achieving the Great Commission mandate of "making disciples"?
- Are congregations open to not only partnering but actually sponsoring and being fully engaged with para-ministries in efforts to "go and make disciples"?
- Are para-ministries seeking *Day's-Decisions* or the making of *Dedicated-Disciples*?
- Are para-ministries willing to rethink their *Level #1* soteriology, so they can re-envision the *Level #2* organizational philosophy, which will bring about a restructured *Level #3* methodology that "makes disciples"?

---

14   My personal experience of working on the staff of two para-ministries that utilized the strategy of camping spanned over two decades. During that time literally hundreds of kids professed faith in Christ at a camp, yet sadly neither of these para-ministries were linked with a local church. I believe this to be a major reason why large numbers of these kids never developed into *Dedicated-Disciples* of Jesus, and sadly, most remain far from Jesus.

Relevance of Soteriology for Sports-Focused Chaplaincy

I. Introduction – Why a Chapter on Sports Chaplaincy

Sports Chaplaincy is also at a crossroad! This crossroad is brought about by two different forces. The first is brought about by those inside Sports Chaplaincy (the current model is proving less and less effective), whereas the second is arising from the outside (discriminatory intolerance for anything Christian). It is my belief that Sports Chaplaincy is in need of contemplative reconsideration of its current model. First however, let's make sure we are talking about the same things.

II. Sports Chaplaincy Defined

A few years ago I was asked to write a chapter as a contributing author for a book on Sports Chaplaincy.[1] The book was published in London with the majority of the manuscript written and edited by people from England. Through that experience I became aware that there are significant differences in how Sports Chaplaincy is done in America and England; and then again, it takes on additional and different shapes in various places throughout the world. The differences aren't only in language and definitions of words or phrases; they are observed more significantly in the philosophical and methodological approach to chaplaincy. While different, it does not necessarily mean either approach is wrong or unBiblical, but the question to be answered has to do with meeting the *4-Fold Evaluative Rubric:* Is Sports Chaplaincy *Strategically-Relevant* and *Efficiently-Effective?*

Most of what follows in this chapter addresses the American model of Sports Chaplaincy; except where specifically referenced. Yet, the following brief overview provides insight into a different international model with the hope it will enable readers to enhance their overall envisioning of the Sports Chaplaincy ministry.[2] While the following definitions and explanations are generalities rather than absolutes; these generalities are by and large accurate in what they describe and assess.

A. English and American Models

Two major distinctions exist between British and American Sports Chaplaincy. The first is who the chaplains are, whereas the second has to do with what the chaplains do.

1. Who the Chaplains Are

The majority of British sports chaplains are first and foremost pastors/ministers who primarily serve a local congregation that enables him/her to

---

1   Linville, Greg. "Sports Chaplaincy and North American Society: Strategies for Winning in the Club House." In Parker, Andrew, Nick J. Watson, John B. White, editors, *Sports Chaplaincy: Trends, Issues, and Debates.* London: Routledge, 2016, p. 32.
2   It is recognized there are a myriad of models that can be found throughout the world, but the scope of this book is limited as is its primary readership and thus this discussion is focused on America and the U.K.

volunteer as a sports chaplain. Usually the pastor's congregation supports, blesses and may even financially underwrite the chapel outreach. Another distinction has to do with the fact that a few national and many club teams have a chaplain, yet few of the chaplains work for a sports ministry such as Christians In Sport (CIS).

This is contrasted with American sports chaplains who for the most part are paid professional Sports Ministers. Many of these chaplains work for one of the various North American sports ministries such as AIA, FCA, PAO or HMI, although a few serve on a church staff. Almost every professional sports team and many college and scholastic teams also have a chaplain.

2. What the Chaplains Do

Chaplains in the U. K. more often provide personal support in social and/or general resource areas rather than spiritual services. While a few may lead a Bible study for a club or team, most of their chaplaincy work focuses on meeting the individual needs of the players they come in contact with. Their outreach is based more in an incarnational and personal approach, rather than in an verbal proclamational model. It would be rare for British sports chaplains to verbally proclaim the Gospel in any Mega-Event setting.

The American Sports Chaplaincy methodology is significantly different. The primary expression of American Sports Chaplaincy is the weekly "chapel" where the major focus is to verbally proclaim the Gospel of Jesus. This 5-15 minute session usually takes place in a locker room or other space in the athletic complex that is provided by the host organization. The American model often includes a separate weekly Bible study for the players. North American chapels and Bible studies are often open to more than just the players including front office personnel, game officials and other stadium workers.

3. Summary of the Two Chaplaincy Models

It was the Irish playwright George Bernard Shaw who said England and the USA are "two countries separated by a common language."[3] Similarly, we are two countries separated by a common ministry name: sports chaplain. There is no right or wrong model here. This brief overview simply articulates the fact there are different expressions of a ministry that are called by the same name, yet can in fact be quite different in methodology.

The concern has not so much to do with the name or who the chaplain is; it has much more to do with underlying beliefs that stem from Level #1 Theological-Truths (what the chaplains and ministries believe) and the organizational Level #2 Philosophical-Principles that emerge from what is believed.

---

3   George Bernard Shaw supposedly made this statement according to *The Treasury of Humorous Quotations*, edited by Evan Esar, English ed. edited by Nicolas Bentley. London: Phoenix House, 1951.

T I M E O U T

A British Perspective on Sports Chaplaincy

It is important to make clear the term Sports Chaplaincy cannot be seen as a homogenous entity. There are many models, types, approaches and intended aims within the generic term Sports Chaplaincy. Different models of Sports Chaplaincy have evolved through the previous decades. A person can serve as a chaplain to various teams (a local school, club or community team; a national team; a college or university team); or as a traveling chaplain to a specific sport's tour (Golf or Tennis); or be available to perform chaplaincy services at major sports events such as the Olympics or World Cup.

The modus operandi of a sports chaplain can vary from conducting pre-game chapel services (a mainly American model) to a much more low-key pastoral role (the norm in the U.K.). The role of the chaplain in sport is to provide pastoral and spiritual support to: Players; coaches; support and administrative staff; and even to sport fans and supporters. Although the work of the chaplain is grounded in a Christian faith perspective, their services are available to adherents of all religious traditions and even to those who espouse no faith at all. Thus, even though the vast majority of sports chaplains would describe themselves as Evangelical Protestants, there are an increasingly large number of professional sportspeople coming to compete in the U.K. from other countries and cultures; and when combined with a continuing decrease in church attendance among the indigenous population; the statement that chaplains serve "those of all religious traditions and those with none" is no theoretical mantra. Chaplains serve the Latin American Roman Catholic soccer player and the Pakistani Muslim cricketer, as well those who would identify themselves as Evangelical Christians.

A phrase which is often used to describe a U.K. chaplain's approach is "pastorally proactive and spiritually reactive." This is an important principle as any overt *Evangelistic-Disciplemaking* activity could easily result in the chaplain's role being terminated. A typical U.K. soccer chaplain might lead a Christmas carol service for the club and conduct weddings and funerals for the club family; but a weekly team chapel service is unheard of. In my experience the main role of the sports chaplain is personal support through a caring presence and a listening ear.

TIMEOUT

A British Perspective on Sports Chaplaincy cont.

An interesting recent development has been increasing levels of co-operation between a club chaplain and a sport psychologist.[1] An important distinction needs to be made here as sports psychologists reporting directly to management, while chaplains are independent of a team's management structures. About 2/3 of the 92 professional English Premier and Football League clubs (soccer) have a chaplain and it's the same number for Rugby League and Rugby Union. Chaplains are typically a local church pastor giving perhaps a day a week to serve the club on a voluntary basis. A number of chaplains have helpfully documented the English football chaplaincy model.[2]

Neither one of the American sports ministries—Athletes in Action/ FCA—has a presence in the U.K., nor is there a similar indigenous ministry organization of comparable size. There are no more than 100 people in the UK who are full-time in Christian ministry to sport. Thus no sports-related, para-ministry organization exists, which has large numbers of staff who could serve as sports chaplains. The one organization which promotes Sports Chaplaincy in the U.K. is aptly called Sports Chaplaincy UK. Founded in 1991, it has never had more than a few staff, relying, rather, on church pastors serving as part-time chaplains in local clubs.

For nine years, (1991-2000) Andrew Wingfield Digby served as spiritual advisor to the England cricket team. This is the only example to my knowledge of a national team having a chaplain. Wingfield Digby told me of his role: "I was there by invitation to offer spiritual support to anyone seeking it. I know that begs a number of questions but I felt it was crucial to stress that I was there by invitation and that the support had to come on someone else's initiative—indicating that they wanted it."

1   Gamble, Richard, Andrew Park, and Denise M. Hill. "Sports Chaplaincy and Psychology." *Sports Chaplaincy: Trends, Issues and Debates*, edited by Andrew Parker, Nick J Watson, and John B White. London, Routledge, 2016. (pp. 182-194)

2   For other books on chaplaincy, see: Rushworth-Smith, David. *Off the Ball*. Basingstoke [Eng.]: Marshalls, 1985; Boyers, John. *Beyond the Final Whistle*. London: Hodder and Stoughton, 2000; Boyers, John. "Manchester United FC." In *Being a Chaplain*, edited by Miranda Threlfall-Holmes and Mark Newitt. London: SPCK, 2011, pp. 81-84; Wood, Stuart. *Keeping Faith in the Team: The Chaplain's Story*. London: Longman Dartman and Todd, 2011; Heskins, Jeffery and Matt Baker, editors. *Footballing Lives*. Norwich [Eng.]: Canterbury Press, 2006

T I M E O U T

A British Perspective on Sports Chaplaincy cont.

There have been people who travelled in a ministry role on the European Golf Tour as well as in track and field. In both cases their presence and role were known to the sport's administrators who seemed positive about what they were doing. However, they had no official title or status. Interestingly none of them used the word "chaplain" to describe their role. There are virtually no sports chaplains in U.K. universities or colleges. The form of chaplaincy in the U.K. most people would be familiar with is hospital chaplaincy. Inevitably Sports Chaplaincy in the U.K. has been influenced by the health sector in its development.

— Stuart Weir
Director of Verite' Sports & U.K. Sports Chaplain, Oxford, England

III. Sports Chaplaincy—Theological, Philosophical & Methodological Questions, Concerns and Proposals

I believe in the strategic value of the general concept of Sports Chaplaincy. However, I also believe Sports Chaplaincy: a) is flawed in its current state; b) has become increasingly ineffective; and thus is c) in need of re-evaluation! This re-evaluation starts with a look at current assumptive Theological foundations

While it is true a solid Christo-centric, Theological case for Sports Chaplaincy has been attempted, sadly this Theological case has not been as deep or thorough as is needed to produce a truly *Strategically-Relevant* and *Efficiently-Effective* model. The good news however, is that a strong Theological foundation for Sports Chaplaincy can be established, and when built upon the integration of the Sports Outreach *Ologies* (ecclesiology; missiology; Christology; and soteriology), this *Level #1 Theological-Truth* foundation will inform and shape a Biblically-based, *Level #2* organizational philosophy from which Sports Chaplaincy can be envisioned, and a *Level #3 Methodological-Model* be created.

Before going on, let me digress for a moment. Generally speaking, I do not question or doubt the relevance of, nor the potential effectiveness of Sports Chaplaincy; I only question its current expression. My overall support for this Gospel-centric strategy is verified by the fact I served as a sports chaplain for many decades including nearly 20 years in professional sports, and multiple decades as a chaplain for various collegiate and scholastic teams. Furthermore I have consistently supported other sports chaplains both prayerfully and financially.

So, yes, I believe in Sports Chaplaincy. Nonetheless, I am troubled by current expressions and models being utilized in the Sports Chaplaincy world. I summarized this concern in the chapter I wrote for a book on Sports Chaplaincy that includes the following quote:

> I believe that there is a more critical issue at stake here; that is, that North American Sports Chaplaincies presently operate in line with what might be described as an ineffective and inefficient Sports Outreach model.[4]

While I won't reiterate all that is in that chapter, I will share here the core of why I believe sports chaplaincy is ineffective and flawed as it is currently practiced: another case of underdeveloped soteriology (as well as a few other underdeveloped *Ologies*). That core of beliefs can be illustrated in a triad that includes: A) No substitute for Church; B) No substitute for radical discipleship; C) No substitute for Jesus.

A. No Substitute for Church

It starts with the first Sports Outreach *Ology*: ecclesiology—the Theology of The Church.

One of the most significant flaws of the current model for sports chaplaincies has to do with the subtle way that providing a Lord's Day religious service at the ball park weens athletes and coaches away from relationship with, and participation in, a local congregation. Not only does it enable a disconnect to develop between the player and a church, it often produces a disconnect between the players and their family. Players attend a 10-15 minute chapel at the ballpark whereas their families participate in a full morning's worship service and Christian education hour at a local church. Over the course of a multi-year career, this fosters and enables a growing, devastating, disconnect between players and their long-term relationship with the major source for special formation and maturation: a local congregation of the universal Church.

B. No Substitute for Radical Discipleship

The second Sports Outreach *Ology* has to do with what we are discussing in this book: soteriology—the Theology of salvation.

Sports chaplains are finding it increasingly difficult to call athletes, especially professional athletes, to true, transformative, discipleship. This difficulty is

---

4   Linville, Greg. Op. cit., p. 32.

typically manifested from three main sources: 1) expectations of host team; 2) expectations of the players, coaches, staff and officials; and 3) personal expectations of the individual chaplains.

1. Expectations of the Teams Chaplains Serve

It should not surprise anyone that professional sports teams are in the business of winning. Thus, teams hire all kinds of people who bring specific assets that help enable winning. These include strength and conditioning coaches; psychologists; medical experts; physical therapists; social workers; marital counselors, and the list goes on. For most teams, chaplains are seen in the same light. The expectation is: chaplains are there to help players be more proficient athletically and thus they make the team more successful.[5]

Therefore, if winning is compromised by anything a chaplain does or says, the entire chaplaincy program will no longer be welcome. Conflicts occur when performance enhancing drugs are recommended; cheating is required; intentionally harming an opponent is demanded; non-adherence to Lord's Day principles is the norm; and/or team commitments always supersede family and church commitments.

Perhaps more disconcerting, host team expectations of chaplains increasingly include not only making chapel services inter-denominational, but more troubling, inter-faith! Meaning, in order to maintain the position/role of team chaplain, the chaplain is expected to include and regularly schedule leaders of other faith groups such as Islamic Imams; Buddhist priests, monks or lamas; Jewish rabbis; Hindu priests, swamis or gurus, etc. [6]

Sports chaplaincies experience many obstacles; some of which challenge the very foundation of being Christ-honoring; Biblically-based and Gospel-centric! This is to say nothing of the expectations of those funding what they believe to be, Christ-honoring outreaches.

2. Expectations of Players, Coaches, Staff and Officials Chaplains Serve

Similarly, sports chaplains encounter the expectations of those whom they have come to serve and reach; many of which revolve around helping athletes and coaches succeed at their sport. Sports in general, and players in specific, tend to be very "superstitious." This often translates into not wanting to do anything to "anger the sports gods." Thus, going to a sports chapel is often viewed as a "talisman," a "rabbit's foot" or "good karma." Sometimes, attending a chapel is even used as an effort to placate a mother, grandfather or spouse. Certainly, some who attend are sincere in their faith and attend to enhance and

---

5   This is another key distinctive between British and American sports chaplains. The expectation in the U.K. is that the chaplains will aid athletes perform better. Whereas this may also be true for American chaplains, theoretically most are more concerned with the spiritual formation of the players they serve.

6   I have attempted to use terminology for the leaders of these religious traditions that are acceptable and honoring, but not being intimately associated with these traditions, I may not have used the proper terminology. I ask for grace if I have used an inappropriate term. Any slight or perceived insult is certainly unintentional.

T I M E O U T

Sports Chaplaincy: A Re-Evaluation Proposal - #1

It is recommended that chaplaincy efforts and outreaches be re-structured around a Monday through Saturday schedule, rather than being focused only as a Sunday ministry.

Specifically, it is recommended that team chaplains start the week by inviting athletes and coaches to join them in participating in Lord's Day worship and Christian education hours in a local congregation; rather than holding a pseudo-substitute service at the ball park called a "chapel."

Then, Monday-Saturday it is hoped chaplains will regularly be present at the ball park to initiate and develop personal relationships with players, coaches, club staff and officials. It is further recommended that chaplains regularly visit the club house, locker rooms, training facilities, sports arenas and fields, seeking to develop personal relationships with all team personnel. These relationships then open up further ministry possibilities such as providing connections to whatever athletes might be in need of, as well as hosting weekly Bible studies, etc.

The bottom line is based in the belief that a prerequisite of discipleship includes commitment to, and participation in, a local congregation of The Church. This ecclesiological-based belief should challenge as well as encourage all sports chaplains to rethink the current model, and reform it to include making significant efforts to connect players and coaches to a local congregation.

May I be so bold as to ask all sports chaplains: if you share the belief that regular membership in, and participation with, a local congregation is the expected norm for a disciple; then what are the specific ways your ministry works to ensure such commitment, relationships, and involvements take place? Just to say you encourage chapel attenders to get involved in a congregation falls far short of intentionally connecting them to a specific church via a specific plan of action.

deepen their faith and walk in Jesus, but I know from personal experience, many of those who attended the chapels I led, did so for less than appropriate motives.

At the very least, even for those who are sincere in their faith, chapel services that are unapologetically Christ-honoring and Biblically-based can create a conflict within those who attend. Players and coaches often feel if they were to live Biblically, their athletic career would suffer which becomes the ultimate conflict for professional coaches and athletes as well as many collegiate players.

3. Personal Expectations of the Chaplains That Serve

Now comes an even more difficult discussion. It has to do with the motivations of the chaplains themselves. I again, quote myself from the previously cited sports chaplaincy book:

> The vast majority of sports chaplains are properly motivated, but even the most conscientious might benefit from a self-evaluation regarding the following issues. Each of us who have served as sports chaplains need to evaluate our motivations for doing so. Is our motivation about being able to associate with elite sports stars honourable? Is sports chaplaincy about accessing game-day tickets, autographs and other sports memorabilia? Unfortunately, it is possible some may compromise the Gospel to maintain the benefits and prestige of being team chaplain. While it is certainly acceptable to be an appreciative recipient of a team's (or player's) graciousness, it is something quite different to compromise the key principles of one's faith to remain as a chaplain.[7]

To that end, I believe it absolutely imperative for each sports chaplain to assess their motivation. Again, from my chapter in the sports chaplaincy book:

> ...the following questions need contemplation by all sports chaplains. Are you willing to remain as chaplain if you do not receive any associated benefits? Are you willing to relinquish your status as chaplain if you are not allowed to freely preach the Gospel and to carry out discussions and teaching in line with Biblical principles? The answers to these (and other) questions determine how effective and efficient US sports chaplaincy will be in the future.[8]

These are not questions that I only ask of others. They are what I ask constantly of myself. They are indeed relevant and necessary to ensure true

7   Linville, Op cit., pp. 36, 37.
8   Linville, Op cit., p. 37.

T I M E O U T

Sports Chaplaincy: A Re-Evaluation Proposal - #2

Beyond the obvious recommendations concerning the individual's motivation for serving as a Sports Chaplain, the main issue to be re-evaluated is: "Is the ultimate goal of the Chaplaincy to 'go and make Disciples?'" It's one thing to try to befriend elite athletes and coaches; it's a further step to seek to get Chapel participants to pray a prayer to receive Jesus as their Savior; it's yet another step to "go and make Disciples."

The real question for Sports Chaplains is: "How do you measure success?" Is it to get an athlete to perform better? Is it being able to verbally proclaim the gospel? Is it praying with someone to receive Jesus as Savior? Is it having someone receive baptism or join a church? Is it to "make a Disciple" and if so, what does that look like and mean? How you and your congregation define success will greatly determine how you organize, administrate and carry out your chaplaincy.

May I be so bold to assume success is the making of disciples....and that includes all of the above: Gospel proclamation; which will eventually lead to praying a prayer of salvation; which should lead to getting baptized; that would include joining a church;... and all of which propels a person to an ongoing Disciple-based life.

If you agree, then how will you transform your Sports Chaplaincy to meet these success objectives?

T I M E O U T

Sports Chaplaincy: A Re-Evaluation Proposal - #3

This proposal may be difficult for some sports chaplains but I believe there is nothing more important than to never, ever, ever, sacrifice the Gospel that is based solely on Christ! Christ has no equal! Christ alone is the Way, the Truth and the Life; and no one comes to the Father except through Him.   Do not be fooled into believing you can compromise in this area and be truly Gospel-centric in your sports Chaplaincy.

The third recommendation is: Rather than reusing the same 10 sports-related passages in the New Testament in your Chaplaincy activities, focus on helping all Chapel participants to see the Christ of the bible; the entire bible. (See The Scoreboard on the next page on The Jesus of the Entire Bible)

Gospel-centric effectiveness. They all have a root concern based upon what salvation actually means and Who it is based on.

C. No Substitute for Jesus

All Sport Outreach *Ologies* are based in Christology.

As has already been stated, the world is moving ever more precipitously towards a Universalist belief that "all roads lead to heaven." This common view is expressed from many preachers and seminar leaders using the following logic (or what I think to be illogic): "we become like the God we envision and thus if we envision a God Who has people burning forever, we become evil, mean-spirited people." The obvious problem with this thinking is that preachers using this kind of argument seek to create God in their image, rather than humbly accepting they were created in God's image—a God Who is not only loving but also just and holy. The new "Theologians" are very much of a millennia-old "enlightenment," and are very much like the children of Israel at the foot of Mt. Sinai. Not liking the God of Moses, they asked Aaron to create a god of gold in an image acceptable to them.[9] It's understandable to expect other religious traditions to be disturbed by Christ's claim to be "the only way;"[10] it's quite different and extremely disconcerting to hear this from preachers, Theologians and professors who claim to be Christian.

---

9   Exodus 32.
10   John 14.6.

Unfortunately, the evidence for the marginalization and even ridicule of all who make Christ the foundation and center of Sports Chaplaincy is becoming more and more obvious and real. Those who humbly and lovingly present the exclusive claims made by Jesus are often perceived to be fools; and condemned as hate-mongering bigots. Sports chaplains who proclaim the exclusiveness of Jesus and His Gospel increasingly experience intolerance and discrimination.

IV. Summary of the Relevancy for Sports-Related Chaplaincy

Sports Chaplaincy is not only Theologically supported and Biblically justifiable but more-so, it can be utilized in such a most profound way as to make it an extremely *Strategically-Relevant* methodology to accomplish Great Commission objectives. However, as currently employed it is not reaching its fullest potential for being *Efficiently-Effective* because of the shallowness of its Theological underpinnings. It is hoped that this will change as leaders within the Sports Chaplaincy community wrestle with the concepts discussed in this book and chapter. As if these issues aren't problematic enough, the following chapter addresses what is a growing concern for anyone desiring to reach those far from Jesus and His Church—encountering a world that is increasingly antagonistic and even violently hostile to all that seeks to share and glorify Christ.

SCOREBOARD

The Jesus of the Entire Bible

- **The Law (Penteteuch)**
  - Anticipates the Need of Jesus
- **The Prophets & Wisdom Books**
  - Predict & Prepare the way for Jesus
- **The Gospels**
  - Reveal the earthly life & teachings of Jesus
- **The Acts of the Apostles**
  - Details how believers preached Jesus and took the Gospel to the world
- **The Epistles**
  - Teach how to live like, and for, Jesus
- **The Revelation**
  - Anticipates the return of Jesus

Relevance of Soteriology in a Multi-Faith World

I. Introduction

There may not be a more relevant chapter in this book!

Individual congregations have been engaged in various forms of Sports Ministry since the 19th century and at the time of writing the modern Sports Outreach Era has entered its 8th decade and yet, never before has The Sports Outreach Community experienced such a time as this.

Whether it is the violent attacks on individual Christians; destruction of church buildings; or other intolerant discrimination against the followers of Jesus, Christianity is being persecuted. Anything having to do with Christianity is under attack by secularism regardless of whether it is benign or virulent. Malevolent anti-Christian religious zealots and adherents to anti-Christian philosophies are all on the attack. In America, at the time of writing, both governmental legislation and judicial fiat continue to chip away at the very existence of religious liberty. Whereas, in other countries two things are occurring: a) where new constitutions are being drafted and signed into law, historically foundational Christian beliefs are being questioned and ridiculed, if not completely outlawed; and b) religious zealots have increasingly buffeted The Church of Jesus Christ including, in some places, having persecuted The Church into oblivion.[1] It is extremely disturbing to hear these stories first hand from those who survive such unthinkable violence.[2]

In the midst of these trends the question needs to be asked: how is The Church, through its local congregations, supposed to carry out its Great Commission mandate? In the face of brutality that threatens life and limb, how are faithful Christian pilgrims to engage their tormentors or ever hope to share the Gospel with them? How to engage and interact with the current culture is what will be addressed in this chapter.

II. Engaging a Multi-faith World

It's one thing to disagree with people who are either adherents of various religious traditions or hold to a non-religious view and philosophy of life; it's quite another to be the recipient of intolerant, mean-spirited and even violent actions when one ascribes to a different faith and/or philosophy. The first is to be expected, even welcomed. The second is unacceptable at any and every level. Yet the question remains: "How should Christians engage and interact with those who are not only far from Jesus and His Church, but more so, are extremely antagonistic towards it?"

---

1   For example, South Africa's fairly recent Constitution includes laws that ban any Christian belief that would uphold the millennia-long held belief on human sexuality, and in many middle-eastern countries Christians have become all but extinct due to violent persecution.

2   I am unable to site specific names and am reluctant to even mention specific countries for fear of jeopardizing the safety of those whose stories I have firsthand knowledge but their experiences would shock and sadden all who hear them.

International Insights
A Stark Reality

Dr. Ed Stetzer suggests that America is shifting from a country of cultural Christianity to one with a more secular world view.[1]

Stetzer reasons that the United States is divided into four religious categories:
- 25% non-Christian
- 25% cultural Christians
- 25% congregational Christians
- 25% convictional Christians

Regardless of the actual statistics, it is generally agreed that the population of people identifying themselves as non-Christian is growing and America continues to move further and further away from holding Christian values.

In that regard, America is becoming ever more like many countries around the world, where Christians are already the minority.

It is for this reason that the SR&F Outreach Ministry has become an ever more strategic bridge that enables local congregations to build relationships with their non-Christian neighbors and friends.

Our international brethren are leading the way in how to reach those who far from Jesus and His Church. Is the American Church willing to learn from them and follow their lead?

— *P.F. Myers – CSRM International Director*

---

1   Stetzer, Ed Christians in the Age of Outrage: How to Bring Our Best When the World Is at Its Worst. Carol Stream, IL: Tyndale Momentum, 2018.
ISBN 978-1-4964-3362-6

The Great Commission mandate remains clear: "go;" "make disciples;" "baptize;" and "teach all that Jesus commanded." How to do this becomes more unclear in the light of all that is currently transpiring, yet one promise in the Great Commission remains: "Behold, I Am with you always, to the end of the age." So then, how do we understand the Great Commission mandate in light of the current trends?

A. Go (The Mission)

The mandate is still to go; regardless of the danger and difficulty. The command is the same for all… "Go to all the world." *Evangelistic-Disciplemaking* assumes "going;" not waiting; not only attracting; not only inviting. The rest of the Great Commission Mandate (baptizing; teaching etc.), cannot not occur unless someone "goes!" The mission of The Church; the mandate for The Church; is to be engaged in evangelistic-based outreach activity. These actions, this mission will accomplish the vision (the making of Disciples.)

1. "Going" To America

For the Division I University Basketball Coach, the overarching call is to win players to Jesus; not win games.[3] Evangelistic goals are still the main call **for those engaging in the business side of sports.** Rather than building a corporate empire, the main call is perhaps best seen in the model of George Williams who consistently encouraged employees and customers to consider accepting Jesus as Lord and Savior, and often prayed with them; even paying their seminary training to become ministers.[4] **For the professional athlete**, it's not about how many autographs you signed or how much you signed your contract for, but rather how many people you influenced to "sign up" to receive Jesus as their Lord and Savior. Does this goal dominate or at least remain a priority for all within the sports world?

This should not be misconstrued to state that the coach, the person in business or world-class athletes should leave those careers and become vocational "evangelists," but rather recognize God has strategically placed them in those vocations for evangelistic purposes. He has placed them in these positions so they are able to first "proclaim the gospel" by being living witnesses of Jesus, which then enables them to "verbally affirm the gospel" by winsomely answering questions about their faith or by stating their faith at appropriate times and places.[5]

---

3   This is not to be misunderstood to say winning games is unimportant! I refer the reader to the first book in this series…*Christmanship: A Theology of Competition and Sport,* where I clearly state winning is an admiral goal and well within the *Christmanship* ethic to strive for. Ultimately however, God will not ask how many games you won, but rather how many people did you "win" to Jesus?

4   George Williams was the founder of the YMCA but remained a life-long business man who was often seen on his knees in his office praying with and for those who worked for him.

5   The concept of Proclamation-Affirmation (proclaiming faith by how one lives and affirming that faith with words) is explained in great depth in the 5th Chapter of the *Fundamentals of Sports Outreach* Book.

For coaches, it is absolutely imperative that they participate weekly in a local congregation's worship, Christian Education offerings and fellowship times! Only then can they actively invite their players to join them in those activities. For those in the business world…besides personally living out one's faith, one strategic option might include providing a professional Chaplain for the business. For elite athletes the "going" would include playing their sport in the Christmanship ethic of playing hard, fair and with joy; and when appropriate, verbally encouraging all whom they play and compete with. Of course, those in business or are world-class athletes are expected to participate each week in a local congregation.

a. Sports Chaplaincy and the American Campus

One indication of the creeping secularization is how some of the sports-related, para-ministries are encountering opposition to their presence on University and High School Campuses. Sometimes this opposition is manifested by schools creating obstacles for para-ministry staff to be on school property. Other times student led chapters/huddles of ministries are denied school sanction. This resistance to anything Christ-centered may be based in benign regulations, but increasingly it stems from discriminatory prejudices aimed at curtailing anything Christian.

There needs to be a two–pronged approach to overcoming these obstacles. First, what is recommended is for those involved to develop relationships - ever-deepening friendships - with school personnel. Secondly, (and only when absolutely necessary), seeking legal protection from discriminatory policies can be utilized.[6]

2. "Going" To The World

Okay, the "going" that has been outlined thus far may be okay for America or the broader western world, but what about those living in a country or region where Christianity is being persecuted into oblivion.

While each and every Disciple of Jesus is mandated to "go," not every follower of Christ is expected to take the Gospel to dangerous places found around the globe! There's a difference between each and every follower of Jesus to be willing to "go" into dangerous and violent situations and actually being called to such a place.

There is a reason why there are age, fitness and, up until more recent times, gender requirements for military participation. War and danger zones are not for the unfit, unprepared and/or those unable to safely and successfully execute what is needed. Similarly, being deployed in dangerous evangelistic environments is recommended for those who are able to handle the rigorous demands of the

---

6   Due to the anticipation of change from the time this was written and published to when it may be read, there is no specific legal group recommended here. What is recommended is a perusal of the CSRM website for an up to date recommended list of legal firms for these kinds of issues.

undertaking. I would further recommend such situations be served by single people who have the skills, professions, knowledge and experiences that can become useful to the culture they seek to bring the Gospel to. A key strategy for successfully navigating these treacherous waters included being able to bring what might seem like secular aid. Physical, emotional, financial and/or psychological aid are more likely able to open doors to communicate the Gospel.

B. Make Disciples (The Vision)

If the mission (the activities/endeavors) of The Great Commission is to "Go," the vision (the reason/purpose/goal) for the mission is to "Make Disciples." Intentionality is the key to accomplishing the vision. In this matter, it is an absolute necessity to be resolute and laser-focused on the Gospel. Yes, seeking justice and reconciliation are hallmarks of true Christianity and thus of vital importance. Yes, all followers of Jesus are called to care about those who suffer, are abused and have physical, social, psychological, emotional and financial needs and yet, even if The Church was to bring about an earthly utopia that ended all injustice, suffering, poverty and pain; the question of eternity still needs to be addressed. The Church would be remiss and extremely negligent if it met all temporal, earthly needs but neglected leading people into a personal and eternal relationship with Jesus. Of course Christians should never underestimate how the very action of meeting the temporal and temporary needs of those they are called to reach, but must never overestimate the benefit of the temporal nature of such short-term, social-justice endeavors. The ultimate vision of the Great Commission is not an earthly utopia but rather an eternal, heavenly reality. The making of Disciples accomplishes both the meeting of temporal and earthly needs as well as eternal, heavenly needs.

C. Baptize (One Key Objective)

If the vision of the Great Commission is the making of Disciples, and its mission is to go into all the world, a key first objective towards the making of Disciples is the baptizing of all who have come into a personal relationship with Jesus. To some this may seem unnecessary and to others it may even seem heretical because they believe salvation does not require baptism. Yet, I believe The Church disregards baptism at its own peril. Furthermore, I believe it is the most misunderstood and under-appreciated aspect of the Great Commission and unless congregations and para-ministries maintain a determined commitment to include baptism as a key component of their disciplemaking efforts, they will never fully experience the pragmatic benefits of this strategy.

As simple, or unimportant as it may seem, I believe admitting baptism is a vital and undeniable component of the Great Commission Mandate. In fact, the Great Commission is not complete without it. In a specific way, it's similar to how the 4th Commandment is often approached. All Disciples of Jesus are commanded to honor the Sabbath. It's not an option! The same is true of baptism. Followers of Jesus must honor the Sabbath and believers in Christ are to be baptized. Again, these two mandates have another similarity. How a person honors the Sabbath has flexibility in expression which leaves some room for discussion and room for various personal applications; but again, not honoring the day is not an option. Likewise, baptism is the norm for all Christians, but there is room for some discussion about the timing, mode and means of that baptism.[7]

In specific, when it comes to baptism there are two main Protestant practices: 1) Believer's-Baptism; and 2) Infant-Baptism. For the purposes of this discussion, it will be assumed that within Protestant expressions both sides of the baptism continuum agree a Biblical practice of the rite of baptism consists of two separate public ceremonies, held at two different times.

1. Believer's-Baptism

On the one end of the spectrum, adherents ascribe to the doctrine of "believer's-baptism" which includes the initial rite of dedicating babies and a later rite of baptism upon a person's profession of faith in Jesus.

The dedication ceremony includes three distinct dedications: a) Parents dedicate their infant/child to the Lord; b) parents dedicate themselves to raising the child according to the bible, in the faith, and in a local congregation; and c) the entire congregation dedicates itself to assisting the parents in the raising the child in the faith.

The second step in the process occurs when the initial ritual of dedication comes to fulfillment years later when the dedicated child is baptized upon their personal profession of faith and conversion (accepting Jesus as Lord and Savior… experiencing a conversion to Christ; entering a personal relationship with Jesus etc.).

2. Infant-Baptism

The second tradition reverses the process described above but maintains the same spirit and purpose. This tradition's initial ritual starts with the baptizing of infants/children as a sign of the covenant of parents and congregation with the child. Infant-baptism anticipates the second step that occurs at a later date in which the person who was baptized as an infant confirms their baptism by making a public proclamation of faith through a second ritual called "confirmation."

The two traditions have more in common than they have in opposition to one another. Both realize the significant importance of two separate ceremonies and the absolute necessity of publicly professing faith in Christ at an age in which

---

7   Once again, this series of books is not designed to present a thorough examination of these doctrines. The presupposition of this book series is that all Christian traditions agree on the importance of Baptism and will leave further and deeper intramural dialogues to other formats.

the commitment to becoming a Disciple of Jesus is more fully comprehended. It is to that end that this discussion now addresses and discusses in relationship to Sports Outreach.

3. Relevance of Baptism for *The Sports Outreach Community*

Regardless of whether the person who has professed faith in Jesus is baptized or confirmed, the thing that is of utter importance is the fact they make a public statement concerning their new found faith. Such a public confession fulfills the demands of the Great Commission and such a public declaration is important to all Sports Outreach endeavors for additional reasons. To that end all SR&F Outreaches are encouraged to adopt a *Level #2 Philosophical-Principle* of organizing their Great Commission endeavors in such a way so as to make a public profession of faith a required part of "making disciples."

If your ecclesiastical community believes in "believer's-baptism" then this step in disciplemaking would be to baptize all who accept Jesus as their Savior. Conversely, if yours is a tradition that confirms a person's "infant-baptism," then the public declaration called "confirmation" is to be expected. The key to both rituals is that they should be incorporated into a congregation's worship service.

The results of these public declarations bring many positives for both the SR&F Outreach Ministry and the broader congregation. Congregations that incorporate these rituals into their Sports Outreach Ministry experience three main encouraging affirmations: a) Overall church growth (as measured by larger church membership, worship attendance and financial contribution…all signs of producing Disciples; b) the encouragement of the faith of all who work and volunteer within the Sports Outreach when they see their efforts resulting in new Disciples; and c) the enhancement of the congregation's leaders, members and attenders understanding and appreciation of the SR&F Outreach Ministry. In short, these public ceremonies provide congregations with the opportunity to celebrate, and this should not be overlooked or underappreciated.

Baptism however, is but one objective and step in the disciplemaking process and it leads to the next step: "teaching them to observe all" of Jesus's commandments.

D. Teach (A Key Strategy)

The final step of the Great Commission is to teach "them to observe all I have commanded you." The teaching of these commands starts with encouraging all who publicly professed faith in Christ to be either baptized or confirmed, but then continues into teaching "all" Christ commands. This is not done quickly, nor haphazardly, but rather systematically over a long period of time and thus I believe this explains why most SR&F Outreach Ministries often neglect this part of the Great Commission! Comparatively, it is much easier, and perhaps more enjoyable to engage in sports, recreation and/or fitness activities than it is to systematically "disciple" someone. It's certainly less time consuming to lead someone in a prayer to receive Christ as Savior, than it is to painstakingly engage new converts in long term activities that make Jesus the Lord of one's life.

Certainly, the broader ministry of a congregation can be expected to play a role in the discipling efforts, but even this is greatly enhanced when the various classes, bible studies and accountability groups are attended together by both the new converts and the SR&F Outreach Ministry leaders and participants who were instrumental in leading the person to Jesus.

The main point of emphasis here however, is the Great Commission is not complete until all of what Jesus commanded is taught to those who have recently come to faith and SR&F Outreach Ministers and Ministries cannot be satisfied with anything less than fulfilling the entire Great Commission which includes going, baptizing and teaching…all of which results in the "making of Disciples." Nothing less fulfills this mandate. So then the question remains…how is this to be done in an increasingly cynical, secularized and intolerant western world and a frightingly violent culture found throughout the world.

E. Obstacles

There are 3 major obstacles that short-circuit the "going to make disciple" in a world so antagonistic to Christ include: 1) fear; 2) lack of *Strategically-Relevant* and *Efficiently-Effective* models; 3) resolute faithfulness to the Gospel.

1. Fear

While understandable, the fear of losing life and limb keeps many from entering many geographic locales within the international mission field. The call to foreign mission is not for the faint of heart, nor those of feeble body or troubled psyche; even in the best of times. That is why anyone contemplating such a call on their life is advised to pursue strong counsel and intense training. Nonetheless, for those called, fear needs to be overcome as modeled by Paul in Corinth when he stayed in dangers way at Corinth.[8] I don't pretend to communicate this is easily done, nor can I promise such faithfulness and obedience will guarantee one's safety; all I can say is it will take brave and hearty souls to take the Gospel into all the world and bring a sense of peace by realizing the Great Comission itself is comforting in recording Jesus's words: "I Am with you always, to the end of the age."[9]

2. Lack of Models

The lack of models shouldn't be surprising but nonetheless it is disappointing. It is recommended that anyone interested in learning about and engaging in relevant and effective models seek out groups such as Uttermost Ministries or other groups that have developed strategic and effective models.

---

8   Acts 18.1-11.
9   Matthew 28.20.

International Insights
The Blow-In, Blow-Up, Blow-Out Model

(While widely practiced it is not recommended)

The problems with *Evangelistic-Disciplemaking* models and SR&F Outreach Ministry go deep. From the West we have passed on an example to our brethren around the world that has produced a church that is a mile long and an inch deep! Unfortunately, the prevalent Western model for Christians lacks any significant depth and thus, disciplemaking is often non-existent. This model emphasizes an evangelism-only focus that allows for a *Days-Decision* by asking people to "pray a prayer and raise their hand" if they want to accept Jesus. The typical Western model concentrates on *Counting-Conversions* rather than "making" life-long, *Dedicated-Disciples*. The process and relationship, if you can call it that, ends with a so called "conversion;" not a Disciple.

Take the example of a short-term mission trip undertaken by a Christian sports team from the West. The team travels to a foreign country for the purpose of playing games against local community teams. At half-time of such games, one or more of the Western team's players share a personal testimony with all in attendance and end with an invitation to all players and fans that "pray the prayer." Those who indicate by the raising of their hands they prayed "the prayer" are then given response cards to fill out and return...sometimes with the promise of a prize to be received. This model is filled with a number of concerns.

First – This model calls into question the motives of those who "prayed the prayer." Have they really accepted Jesus or are they doing it with the hope of receiving a prize or having contact with and blessing from the visiting foreigner?

Second - Unless the international team is working with a local congregation, or with those who are in the process of planting a congregation, the chances for follow-up are non-existent, and thus, the chances of growing a true Disciple is greatly reduced.

Therefore it is recommended for all engaged in international SR&F Outreach Ministry to re-evaluate how they measure their *Success-Statistics*. Is what is being done a *Blow-in; Blow-up and Blow-out* methodology where the individual or team comes in; plays a game; "preaches" the Gospel; pats themselves on the back for the

International Insights
The Blow-In, Blow-Up, Blow-Out Model cont.

great job THEY have done; and then leaves for the next game or event?

If so, it's time to re-envision such a methodological approach from a fuller and deeper understanding of the Theology of salvation. This will then inform how a new philosophy of ministry will be organized, out of which a new model of ministry will emerge that truly empowers local congregations for disciplemaking; building the local church; and allowing sports people to use their gifting and calling to expanding God's Kingdom.

— *P.F. Myers, CSRM International Director*

The International Insights Side Bar on starting on page 108 is written by CSRM's Director of International Ministry P. F. Myers who in my estimation is a modern day Apostle Paul having equipped local church Sports Outreach Ministers in over 90 countries and in his side bar he shares the current ineffective model.[10]

3. Resolute Faithfulness to the Gospel

A subtle pitfall often sneaks up on the missionaries who are attempting to be relevant to those they are trying to reach. What begins as an attempt to initiate relationships with people of other religious backgrounds sometimes shifts to accommodating one's belief about the Gospel.

Whether the SR&F Outreach Missionary is reaching out to a secularized *De-Churched* American (someone who has only a nominal relationship in a religion or a devout cleric of another religion), even the most well-intentioned Christ-follower can succumb to the pressure of being "open-minded," and to not be so "narrow-minded." There is a great attraction to believe "all faiths lead to heaven."

It's much less disturbing to change one's belief about hell than it is to communicate to new made friends that unless they become a Disciple of Jesus they will spend eternity separated from God in hell. Holding to a resolute faithfulness to the Gospel becomes increasingly difficult as the life, heart and mind of those of other religious traditions are realized, understood and appreciated.

Thus, one of the most disturbing realities of incarnational *Evangelistic-Disciplemaking* becomes clear when the evangelist encounters a person of

---

10   Connect with other models via the CSRM website.

TIME OUT

What Color Is The Gospel?

Many places around the globe have made "proselytizing" illegal. What this most often means is that anyone who attempts to share the Gospel of Jesus Christ can be arrested, prosecuted, imprisoned; or worse. While in some of these countries it is illegal to initiate a conversation that would lead to a Gospel proclamation, Christians are legally allowed to respond to questions asked of them concerning their faith in Christ. In other locales initiating spiritual conversations might not be illegal but considered impolite and offensive.

So in these situations how can followers of Jesus verbally communicate their faith within both the spirit and the letter of the law of their land? One unique strategy the Sports Outreach Community has created is via a "Power Ball."

The power ball can be used for any sport such as volleyball, basketball or rugby, although the most prevalent would be soccer due to its global prominence. The only difference between a normal sports ball and the power ball is that the power ball is multi-colored rather than the normal orange of basketball or white/black of a soccer ball. Here's how it works...

First the follower of Jesus befriends other athletes who play their sport. Second, the Christian begins to pray for their new friends; specifically that the Lord would open the heart of their new friends to warmly receive the message of the gospel. Third, the follower of Jesus begins to use the colored ball during kick arounds and practices and waits for someone to ask about the unique color-scheme of the ball; all the while living in a way that truly honors Jesus and loves their teammates. The next hoped for step occurs when the question concerning the colors on the ball. It is then believers verbally share the Gospel by explaining the colors found on the ball...

Blue – God came from a blue heaven...

Green – To a green Earth...

Red – To shed His red blood...

Gold – So we can be reconciled to Him and wear a gold crown

another religion who is sincere in their faith and rejects Jesus and claims their religion is all they need. In an effort to remain friends with those of other religious communities the Christian begins to "soften" the exclusive claims of Jesus being the only way. This thinking progresses when the follower of Jesus witnesses the life of their new friends...lives that often reflect many moral and spiritual positives and they begin to reason... "Can Jesus really mean these folks will not inherit eternal life...after all, they are good, moral, and even religious people?" The end result of the progression of experience and thinking is the "evangelist" no longer evangelizes but succumbs to a world view that believes Christ is only one way to heaven, not the only way.

So how can this all be summarized?

III. Summary and Challenge

Summary: Each individual in the world needs Jesus, and the world needs more Disciples of Jesus who bring hope, joy, peace and love to all! Yet, the world is increasingly antagonistic to Jesus, and the Christian Church is being persecuted at unprecedented levels; often in horribly violent ways. As a result, The Church finds itself needing to re-evaluate the *Evangelistic-Disciplemaking* efforts it is currently engaged in. The Church is also in need of a recommitment of both its individual members and congregations resolve to reach those far from Jesus.

Will *The Sports Outreach Community* rise up to meet this challenge? My prayer is that "we" will. My efforts to that end include the writing of this book. I offer it as a clarion call for The Church to engage in *Strategically-Relevant* and *Efficiently-Effective* ways; especially to those individuals and countries that are most antagonistic to anything Christ-oriented.

Challenge: Are you called into "all the world?" Will you and your congregation recommit yourselves to the goal of taking the Gospel to the world in our generation....even a hostile and violent world? Fulfilling the Great Commission has never been more necessary.

Summary of Soteriology in Relationship to SR&F Outreach

I. Where We Are

We are now at the end of the fourth book in the Institutes of Sports Outreach Book Series. So far we have established:

➢ A basic *Level #1 of Theological-Truth* and Apologetics for Sports Outreach in Book #1
➢ A *Level #2* overview of organizational *Philosophical-Principles* in book #2
➢ Two of the specific *Sports Outreach Ologies Level #1 Theological-Truths*
    ➢ Ecclesiology in book #3
    ➢ Soteriology in this book #4

The case has been made that while a solid Theological and Biblical defense of competition, sport and Sport Outreach can be made, there remains a significant concern about the effectiveness of the current expressions and models of Sports Outreach Ministry. Whereas, the Theological/Biblical justification for the strategic tool of sport, recreation and fitness is no longer questioned, the *Ologies* of *The Sports Outreach Community* are helping to establish why this tool is not as pragmatically effective as it could be. This book in particular has pointed out how important the understanding of soteriology is to ensure a congregation's (and for that matter, to ensure the entire *Sports Outreach Community's*) *Success-Statistics* are valid, authentic and ever increasing. What has been produced so far anticipates more to come in future books.

II. Reviewing the Major Assertions Made in this Book

What follows is an overview of the major points that this book has added to the development of the *Level #1 Theological-Truths* that undergird the *The Sports Outreach Community.*

A. The Sports Outreach Community is Struggling to be Effective

The first point this book made was really a reiteration of previous assertions: that although the tool of SR&F Outreach Ministry is valid and holds promise, it is falling short of its potential to effectively reach those who are far from Jesus and His Church.

B. Going to make Disciples is the Essence of The Great Commission

The second major point of this book has to do with emphasizing The Great Commission is only truly realized and fulfilled with the "making of disciples." This emphasis is put in contrast with efforts described as *Counting-Conversions* that seek what is termed a *Day's-Decision* (referencing a short-term, passing fancy) rather than laboring to "go and make" life-long, *Dedicated-Disciples.*

C. Re-evaluating *Success-Statistics*

The third point of this book introduces the concept of *Success-Statistics.* The most relevant aspect of *Success-Statistics* has to do with helping congregations establish authentic criteria for determining the effectiveness of their outreach. This concept challenges a prevailing notion that a congregation's goal is based on the *Counting-Conversions* of *Day's-Decisions*. Rather, the goal should be to "go and make disciples."

D. The Impact of Cheap Grace

The fourth point of this book addresses the issue that a dominant reality throughout evangelical Christianity is the cheapening of what it means to become a disciple of Jesus. Characterized by the theme introduced by Dietrich Bonhoeffer, the concern is that the Church, in an effort to win people to Christ, has presented a "watered-down" version of the authentic Gospel to those very people. The result therefore is that while the reported numbers of people making a *Day's-Decision* about faith in Christ are huge, the real numbers of people who become life-long, *Dedicated-Disciples* are much lower. This then explains why so many congregations report large numbers of "conversions" but never experience any growth in their membership; participation in worship, Christian education opportunities or the tithes and offerings they receive.

E. Stating the Biblical Foundation for Soteriology

The fifth point of this book relies upon and assumes a classic, orthodox soteriology for encouraging *The Sports Outreach Community* to maintain a truly Biblical focus on the *Trilogy of Gospel-Centricity* (The centrality of: Jesus; the Church; and the Great Commission); and to the *Singular-Commitment-Cost* that true discipleship demands. It re-emphasizes: a) the strategic wisdom of basing all *Evangelistic-Disciplemaking* efforts of the Church through its local congregations; b) the absolute necessity of Christ; and c) it also mandates calling those far from Jesus to true discipleship by avoiding "cheap grace." Establishing and embracing such a soteriological foundation will greatly expand and enhance a congregation's Gospel effectiveness.

F. Obstacles to Effective Outreach

Major obstacles for effective SR&F Outreach Ministry make up the sixth major point of this book. A vital revelation for congregations trying to reach those who are far from Jesus and His Church is understanding how to avoid either of the two extremes of how local churches often approach competition (*Competition-Gone-Berserk* or *Competition-Gone-Soft*). Both are counter-productive to their overall goals and sport, if it is not done well, can be the very thing that actually keeps a person from becoming a disciple. In addition, many congregations and sports-related, para-ministries create an additional obstacle by not understanding and upholding a strong commitment to a Lord's Day Theology that includes the day being a major pillar for disciplemaking activities.

G. Easy Believism & The Carnal Christian

Two additional points make up the seventh major point of this book. Both are related to a particular aberration of soteriology. The first is a deeper look at the impact of what Bonhoeffer described as cheap grace. The second highlights the disastrous results of the teaching that Jesus only need be a Savior, not Lord.

H. Sports Chaplaincy Model Questioned

The major concern about the eighth major point of this book is not whether or not Sports Chaplaincy is a good strategy, but rather, the question has to do with its current *Methodological-Model*. In England, the concern lies in the fact that the current model is prone to rarely call sports figures to a personal faith in Jesus. Likewise, the American model is of concern because of lack of calling athletes and coaches to become intimately involved in a local congregation.

I. Multi-Religious World

The last major point in this book centers on how the Sports Outreach Community has not sufficiently envisioned, planned for and engaged in a *Strategically-Relevant* outreach that can truly be *Efficiently-Effective* in its *Evangelistic-Disciplemaking* endeavors in a multi-religious and increasingly secular world.

III. Restating Major Recommendations

The following section serves as a review that briefly restates the major recommendations made throughout this book about the major points outlined in the previous section of this chapter.

A. Getting Soteriology Right

The first and main recommendation of this book is for Church and congregational leaders to wrestle with, and establish, their Theology of salvation, guide and subsequently develop a relevant plan for how their soteriology should inform how they will organize their ministry. Unless Church and congregational leaders intimately know what they want their *Success-Statistics* to measure, they will be unable to envision and organize any effective outreach ministry.

B. Getting *Success-Statistics* Right

Clarifying what *Success-Statistics* actually measure is the step that follows establishing the soteriology of a ministry. It is recommended this clarification goes deeper and further than pursuing people to make a *Day's-Decision* and *Counting-Conversions* in favor of laboring to help those far from Jesus and His Church to *Become* life-long *Dedicated-Disciples*.

C. Getting Competition Right

A strong recommendation is to get a solid handle on *Christmanship* as a basis of congregational competition and sport. This will mitigate or even negate any negative repercussions that might occur when competition is out of control

(*Competition-Gone-Berserk)* and/or its strength (*Competition-Gone-Soft)* is not maximized.

D. Getting The Lord's Day Right

Another strong recommendation is to get a solid handle on the doctrine of The Lord's Day, and how honoring it, can catalytically empower the *Evangelistic-Disciplemaking* efforts of a congregation.

E. Getting The Para-Ministry Right

Sports-related, para-ministries are strongly recommended to rethink their soteriology in three specific ways: a) What they communicate to their athletes and coaches about Jesus being not only Savior but also Lord, which includes; b) connecting each athlete and coach to a local congregation; and c) basing their ministry in and through a local congregation.

F. Getting Sports Chaplaincy Right

There are three proposals when it comes to American Sports Chaplaincy: 1) Adapt the schedule and format of the chaplaincy; 2) adapt what is measured; but 3) never adapt the Gospel of Jesus. Adapting the schedule and format means to change from only providing a Lord's-Day-morning-service in favor of having athletes attend services with a local congregational body, and then engaging in other chapel activities throughout the other six days of the week. Adapting what is measured has to do with "making disciples" rather than *Counting-Conversions.* Never adapting the Gospel entails never succumbing to the pressures to modify or change the claims of Jesus being the only way to be "saved."

G. Getting The Outreach To The World Right

The main proposal about going to the American campus and/or other areas dominated by progressive, humanistic-secularism, is to work hard at developing relationships rather than engaging in more confrontational activities.

The main proposal for going to the rest of the world, especially those places where Christianity is highly persecuted or ill-thought of, is to be extremely wise and sensitive to the existing culture and yet remain thoroughly committed to the Great Commission tenets of: a) going; b) baptizing; and c) teaching all that Jesus commanded. This assumes disciples are painstakingly made with much effort and often through great sacrifice.

IV. Where Do We Go From Here?

The ultimate objective for the Institutes of Sports Outreach Book Series (of which this book is the fourth); is to catalytically undergird and empower the efforts of thousands of SR&F Outreach Ministers the world over, who daily attempt to: "go and make disciples." This objective is accomplished by basing all content in the book series upon the 3-*Tier Paradigm...*

> **Level #1 *Theological-Truths: Christo-centric Theological foundations***
>> The *Why* we do What we do
>>> How we think
>>> How we determine what we believe
>>> How we envision Outreach Ministry
> **Level #2 *Philosophical-Principles: Biblically-Based operations***
>> The *Who, When & Where* we do What we do
>>> How we organize
>>> How we administrate
>>> How we implement our core values
> **Level #3 *Methodological-Models: Strategically-Relevant & Efficiently-Effective Activities***
>> The *What* we do
>>> How we carry out missional programs
>>> How we carry out activities, leagues, clinics, classes

So, we are progressing in our pursuit of fully *Informing, Instructing and Inspiring* all SR&F Outreach Ministers who strive to mobilize their congregations to reach those far from Jesus and His Church. This book is the second that addresses the *Level #1 Theological-Truth* tenets of *The 3-Tier Paradigm* and the next book in this series continues the Theological discussion as it addresses the Theology of the mission of The Church—missiology. These books will be followed by additional entries into the Sports Outreach Institute book series that will explore more *Level #2 Philosophical-Principles* and *Level #3 Methodological-Models.*

I leave the final word to my colleague and dear brother P. F. Myers in his International Insights that follow.

International Insights
A Final Question

After the stoning of Stephen, in Acts 8:1 we read:
"And there arose on that day a great persecution against the church in Jerusalem, and they were all scattered throughout the regions of Judea and Samaria, except the apostles."

Of course, what went with those persecuted believers was the Gospel that was proclaimed and lived out!

Francis Chan relates an account of speaking with a church leader in China who shared five pillars to the growth of the house church movement. (Chan, Francis. *Letters To The Church*. Colorado Springs, CO: David C. Cook, 2018. Pp. 134f)

These pillars are:
1. A deep commitment to prayer
2. A commitment to the Word of God
3. A commitment to every member sharing the Gospel
4. Regular expectation of miracles
5. Embracing suffering for the glory of Christ

From this I invite you, your church and your SR&F Outreach Ministry to compare yourselves against these pillars. In fact I implore each of us to do so—that is if we want to be most effective for the Gospel.

Questions for us all include: How important is prayer and teaching God's Word? Are we discipling leaders and converts to share their faith? Are we expecting God to move beyond our own abilities and experiences to even do miracles in our lives and in the lives of those we are serving?

continued on page 120

International Insights
A Final Question cont.

In addition, regarding persecution, maybe it has not come to us yet, but is that because we are not boldly proclaiming Jesus? The reality is as our world is becoming increasingly antagonistic against Christianity, and the more we proclaim Jesus the more likely persecution will come.

I am sure that some of the five pillars are more relevant for you and your ministry at this time, but in the future all will most certainly find their place. To my point, we can learn a lot from our persecuted brothers and sisters around the world. If persecution is the seed of the Church (some would say its very lifeblood); then it stands to reason those who are persecuted for "playing sports with a purpose" (for *Evangelistic-Disciplemaking*) are engaged in activities that are the very lifeblood of SR&F Outreach Ministry!

I am convinced there is no better strategy than SR&F Outreach Ministry that God has given His Church today. It is a strategy that can be and in fact, is being used effectively in even the most difficult places and under the most difficult circumstances to build His Church. No matter where you are ministering in SR&F Outreach Ministry; take note and keep pressing on!

— P.F. Myers, CSRM International Director

Postscript

Any book about soteriology would not be complete without a specific invitation to all who read this book to accept Jesus as their personal Lord and Savior.

To some this might come as a surprise because they assume anybody reading this book would only do so because they are already disciples of Jesus. After all, they reason, the target audience is Sports, Recreation and Fitness Ministers and thus it would be assumed such people are already Christians. While this is usually the case, there are times the person hired for these ministries is so hired because of athletic skills and background. The faith of the new minister is either assumed or never seen as the major criteria for being hired. This is why I have occasionally met someone who bears the title of Sports Minister but hasn't yet made a profession of faith in Jesus. These folks are always wonderful people; are not opposed to a Christian ethic of sport; support praying for safety etc. before games held at the congregation's ministry site; and yet they have never truly professed Christ as their Lord.

A second category of Sports Outreach Ministers are those who may have come to a new realization while reading this book. Prior to reading the book they have always assumed they were a Christian but something in the book caused them to see things in a different light or revealed something they had never realized or knew before. For example, they may have read the sections about "cheap grace" or what it means to be a *Dedicated-Disciple* and felt the Holy Spirit nudging them to evaluate their own faith.

Regardless of who or why, this Postscript is written to warmly invite each reader to reflect on their own life and faith....or lack of it. For those who have never received Jesus as their Lord and Savior, or for those who are seeking an assurance of their faith, I offer the following.

Diagnostic Questions

1. Have you ever said yes to Jesus…making a *Day's-Decision* to accept Him as your Savior
    a. If so, then move on to question #2
    b. If not, why not do so right now
2. If you have either before, or just now, accepted Jesus as your Savior, have you ever acknowledged Him to be the Lord of your life by committing to become a *Dedicated-Disciple* of His
    a. If so, move on to question #3
    b. If not, commit right now to begin engaging in the following
3. Have you ever been baptized or confirmed
    a. If so, then move on to question #4
    b. If not, schedule a time to meet with your Pastor to discuss making your profession of faith in Jesus public and then schedule the Lord's Day you will do this
4. Have you ever engaged in a basic Discipleship course that covers foundational Christian doctrine and practice
    a. If so, move on to question #5
    b. If not, commit now to take part in your congregation's discipleship class
5. Are you committed to regular, consistent, personal and corporate worship experiences and bible study
    a. If so, move on to question #6
    b. If not put on your calendar and participate in the following spiritual formation activities
        i. Personal
            1. Daily bible study (deeper than only reading a verse or chapter)
            2. If married… a daily bible reading with your spouse
            3. If a parent of children…a daily bible reading with your family
        ii. Small group weekly participation in
            1. A men's or women's bible study
            2. A Sunday School class
            3. If married…a couple's bible study
        iii. Corporate participation in
            1. Weekly - A Lord's Day Worship
            2. Seasonal, yearly or special congregational activities

6. Are you committed to maintaining a prayer journal
   a. If so, move on to question #7
   b. If not commit yourself to beginning a maintaining a prayer journal that includes
      i. Praise of the Lord
         1. Including recognizing and thanking Him for His Holiness and for the blessings He brings your way
      ii. Prayer for His Church to be expanded and enhanced
         1. Including who it is He wants you to
            a. Reach for Him
            b. Love and minister to in His name
      iii. Prayer for your needs and desires
         1. Including health, finance, anxieties, concerns, relationships etc.
      iv. Confess any sins and ask for His forgiveness
         1. Including considering anyone you need to forgive and make a relationship right with
      v. Prayer for God's faithfulness to you and His leading of you
         1. Including God's protection from danger, temptation and evil
7. Are you committed to reaching others for Jesus
   a. If so...I hope this list serves as an encouragement to you in knowing you are truly a life-long *Dedicated-Disciple* of Jesus
   b. If not, commit yourself to...
      i. Asking God who it is He wants you to reach for Him
      ii. Pray for these people and begin to envision how you can love and serve them in the hope they will one day trust Jesus as their own personal Lord and Savior

Final Thoughts

The contents of this Postscript should not be misinterpreted to communicate that you can earn your salvation by attending to each of the seven questions. I state it clearly: Salvation comes by "faith alone" and is not attained by "works."

However, we also know that salvation is never only faith alone without any subsequent works. Rather, a *Day's-Decision* is the first and necessary step of becoming a *Dedicated-Disciple.*

Therefore, since the Great Commission mandate Jesus gave was to: go; make disciples; baptize; and teach all He had commanded; then soteriology (a Theology of salvation) is incomplete unless each of the things He commanded become reality in the lives of all disciples of Jesus.

If you have never received Jesus as your Lord and Savior, I warmly encourage you to do so right now.

Glossary

1-*Foundational Purpose of Sports Outreach*
The first transferable concept and the guiding principle of *The Sports Outreach Community*. It describes the end goal of *The Community*: making *Dedicated-Disciples* of Jesus Christ.

2-*Dysconnects of Sports Outreach*
The second transferable concept describes and defines the two hurdles SR&F Outreach Ministries encounter in reaching those far from Christ and His Church. The first dysconnect has to do with attracting people from the general community in which they live, to specific local church SR&F activities. The second dysconnect has to do with moving people from the SR&F activities to the broader congregational activities including becoming active participants in traditional worship and Christian Education opportunities.

3-*I's*
The *3-I's* form a *Re-sourcing; Re-training* & *Re-energizing* continuum for fully equipping SR&F Outreach Ministers for the purpose of empowering them to envision, plan for, organize, administrate and evaluate a truly *Strategically-Relevant* & *Efficiently-Effective, Evangelistic-Disciplemaking* Sports Outreach Ministry.
• *Inform* – has to do with the creation, production and distribution of Re-sources that are: Christo-centric *Level #1 Theological-Truths*; Biblically-Based *Level #2 Philosophical-Principles*; and *Level #3 Methodological-Models*.
• *Instruct* – has to do with Re-training SR&F Outreach Ministers in how to most effectively utilize and employ the Re-sources that have been created, produce and distributed.
• *Inspire* – has to do with Re-energizing SR&F Outreach Ministers with new motivations and inspirations for reaching those far from Jesus and His Church and also has to do with developing ongoing, personal, mentoring, relationships that enables SR&F Outreach Ministers to become fully equipped for successful Great Commission endeavors.

3-Tier Paradigm Organizational Structure

The third transferable concept outlines the organizational structure of SR&F Outreach Ministries. Based upon three levels, it builds from a foundation of how to think (Theologically); which shapes and informs how to organize (philosophically); out of which what to do (methodology) emerges. Moving from *Why* a SR&F ministry exists to *When, Where* and for *Whom* it is organized to What is done; this organizational structure ensures *Strategically-Relevant* and *Efficiently-Effective* SR&F Outreach Ministry.

4-Fold Evaluation Rubric

The fourth transferable concept describes the four necessary components for ensuring a SR&F Outreach Ministry will accomplish its goals and objectives which include being Strategic; Relevant; Efficient and Effective.

5-B's Process of Sports Outreach

The fifth transferable concept explains the process of developing a *Repetitive-Redemptive-Relational* ethos and culture within SR&F Outreach Ministry for the purpose of making *Dedicated-Disciples* of Jesus. It outlines how a SR&F can envision, plan for and implement an effective outreach ministry.
- *Belong*
- *Believe*
- *Baptize*
- *Behave*
- *Become*

7-Continuums of Tension of the Sports Outreach Movement

The sixth transferable concept outlines the seven most important Theological and philosophical issues confronting The Sports Outreach Movement as it enters its 7th decade.

Accommodation

One of four classical responses and reactions embraced by sport-related individuals who encounter the dilemma of integrating faith and their sport. It describes those who choose sport over faith but try to hold on to both.

Blow-In; Blow-Up; Blow-Out

This *Level #3 Methodological-Model* consists of: a) an American sports team *Blowing-In* to a specific community within a foreign country to play a game against a local or national team; b) having one or more of the athletes verbally share the Gospel (*Blow-Up*) and ask for those in attendance to "accept Jesus;"

and then c) *Blow-Out* to the next stop on the short term mission trip. This phrase was first used by Sports Outreach Ministry Pioneer Rodger Oswald who used it to describe the essence of what all too often occurs when American sports teams engage in short term international mission trips. It is based on a soteriology (Theology of salvation) that believes the mission's goal is fulfilled and accomplished when a person "raises their hand" or "prays a prayer" with limited regard to "making disciples" and connecting those being reached with a local congregation.

Building-with-Leaders
Building-with-Leaders is a *Level #2 Philosophical-Principle* that emphasizes the importance of investing in leaders and their development for the ultimate purpose of achieving *Strategically-Relevant* and *Efficiently-Effective* SR& F Outreach Ministry. This philosophy is the true bed-rock of SR&F Outreach Ministry but should not be used to dismiss the importance of constructing and maintaining high quality athletic and fitness facilities, which greatly enhance and expand local church outreach efforts. *Building-with-Leaders* is a philosophy that seeks to recruit, *Re-Source*; *Re-Train* and *Re-Energize* local church volunteers to build effective *Redemptive-Repetitive-Relational* opportunities with friends, family members and associates for the purpose of *Evangelistic-Disciplemaking*. This phrase is often partnered with its corollary: *Leading-with-Buildings*.

Capitulation
One of four classical responses and reactions embraced by sport-related individuals who encounter the dilemma of integrating faith and sport. It describes those who not only choose sport over faith but totally abandon their faith in favor of sport.

Christmanship
One of three philosophical approaches to competition and sport; *Christmanship* describes a laser-focused and Biblically-based, Christ-honoring ethic of engagement with sport. As compared with gamesmanship that espouses the highest ethic is to win; or sportsmanship which emerges from a philosophy rooted in humanistic relativism and ends with an ethic of fair play etc.; *Christmanship* is an ethic that outlines how to engage in sport for the glory of God and in ways that honors all *co-competitors*.

Co-Competitors
A term in the Christmanship Ethic used to describe individuals who play on other teams. This descriptive term is used rather than words such as opponent, adversary or enemy.

Competition-Gone-Berserk

Competition-Gone-Berserk is a phrase used to describe how some local church Sports Ministries have completely abdicated on creating a culture of Biblically-based competition (*Christmanship*). Unchecked and unsupervised competition often results in participants experiencing such a negative competitive environment that they choose to not only leave the church league, but more significantly, they decide to have nothing to do with the congregation that sponsors the league. Whether born out of a total lack of any Theological structure for competition and sport, or from an underdeveloped *Level #1 Theological-Truth* of competition, the end result of *Competition-Gone-Berserk* is the same…a lost opportunity to reach those far from Jesus and His Church.

Competition-Gone-Soft

Competition-Gone-Soft is a phrase used to describe how some local church sports ministries seek to greatly curtail or totally eliminate competition within all of their leagues and games. This approach is usually born out of an underdeveloped *Level #1 Theological-Truth* that believes competition is intrinsically and inherently evil. This underlying Theology leads to a local church sport outreach ministry envisioning and developing a ministry structure that doesn't reward Godly competition and even penalizes anything bordering on competition. Sadly, the organizational structures that emerge out of such *Level #2 Philosophical-Principles* lead to *Level #3 Methodological-Models* that are not appealing to large segments of those who are far from Jesus and His Church; and thus do not attract them to participate in any of the outreach programs a congregation offers. There are however, specific sports outreaches that are rightfully designed to create less intense competition: a) Low impact volleyball for beginners; b) slo-break basketball for seniors; c) basketball clinics for pre-schoolers; and d) various fellowship leagues of all ages. Nonetheless, for the most part, non-competitive sporting activities do not attract or keep people involved. Any local church that seeks to "go and make disciples" of athletes is encouraged to develop a culture of Biblically-based competition (*Christmanship*) that will be managed so as to appeal to, and attract, competitors to participate…all with the end goal of winning them to Jesus.

Core Values

Whereas *Theological-Truths* define and describe the *Why*; *Philosophical-Principles* define and describe the When, Where & with Whom; and *Methodological-Models* describe and define the What of the 3-Tier Paradigm; the Core Values define and describe the How of the *3-Tier Paradigm*. Core Values have to do with creating an environment of organizational and administrative excellence; an atmosphere of warmth, love and encouragement; and a culture of integrity, punctuality, efficiency and safety. Core Values consider how participants in SR&F activities feel; and are the bedrock of "proclaiming" the Gospel through the fleshing out the Great Commandment.

Counting-Conversions

Counting-Conversions is a phrase used to summarize how many congregations, denominations, missions and ministries determine the effectiveness of their *Evangelistic-Disciplemaking (Success-Statistics)* endeavors. It describes the fact that many ministries and churches believe evangelistic success is complete and done whenever a person "converts" to Christianity (what is often called getting them "saved"). This end goal of "getting a person saved" is evidenced by one or more of the following: a) Raise a hand at the end of a team huddle; b) pray a prayer with a coach or other evangelist; or c) fill out a card in response to a *Platform-Proclamation* of the Gospel at a *Mega-Event*. *Counting-Conversions* is linked with the concept of endeavoring to have people make a *Day's-Decision* for Jesus, rather than seeking to "make" life-long *Dedicated-Disciples* of those who far from Jesus and His Church. The key distinction is the ultimate goal of such endeavors. Is the end and final goal to get a person to make a decision or become a disciple?

Day's-Decision

Day's-Decision is one of the *"Double D's"* of soteriology. It is used in discussions concerning topics such as salvation, evangelism and outreach. It is used in tandem with *Dedicated-Disciple* and describes the pragmatic end result of SR&F Outreach Ministries. Based in a *Level #1 Theological-Truth* of soteriology, it is based in a simplistic Theology of evangelism that strives to get a person to "raise a hand;" "pray a prayer;" or "fill out a response card." Any of these end results indicate a person accepted Jesus on a particular day. While proponents of this approach to evangelism would never say they would discourage participation in a local congregation; nor would they state discipleship to be unimportant; nonetheless, this phrase describes those congregations and ministries that tend to not incorporate ongoing disciplemaking methodologies into their overall evangelistic endeavors.

Dedicated-Disciple

Dedicated-Disciple is one of the *"Double D's"* of soteriology. It is used in discussions concerning topics such as salvation, evangelism and outreach. It is used in tandem with *Day's-Decision* and describes the pragmatic end result of SR&F Outreach Ministries. Based in a *Level #1 Theological-Truth* of soteriology, it is based in the belief that *Evangelistic-Disciplemaking* consists of not only getting a person to "raise a hand;" "pray a prayer" or "fill out a response card." This philosophy believes it is equally important to engage all who have accepted Jesus as Lord and Savior in disciplemaking activities to ensure full spiritual maturity. While proponents of *Evangelistic-Disciplemaking* would never say a *Day's-Decision* is unimportant; nor would they state accepting Jesus as personal Lord and Savior to be irrelevant; they seek to pragmatically incorporate ongoing disciplemaking methodologies into their overall evangelistic endeavors.

Efficiently-Effective
Paired with *Strategically-Relevant*, it is the second half of the *4-Fold Evaluative Rubric*. Efficiently-Effective suggests the criteria congregations need to help assess and determine whether or not a local church SR&F Outreach Ministry is actually accomplishing its goal of making disciples. It defines and describes ultimate effectiveness; and also communicates the importance of basing the organization and administration of SR&F Outreach Ministry within a strong stewardship ethic.

External Motivational Influences of Competition (EMIC)
EMIC - describes the pressures of competing because of, with, or against external forces such as time, obstacles, challenges of weather or other natural causes, courses (golf, race, etc.) and/or other human beings.

Evangelistic-Environments
Evangelistic-Environments describe one of the key aspects of the Core Values of the *3-Tier Paradigm*. The ultimate goal of a SR&F Outreach Ministry is to create a winsomely attractive and warm environment that facilitates opportunities for congregational members to build relationships with friends, associates and family members for the purpose of having evangelistic conversations.

Evangelistic-Disciplemaking
In essence this describes how to reach and disciple those far from Christ and His Church. This term uniquely defines the *1-Defining Purpose* of *The Sports Outreach Community*. It assumes that "to go and make disciples" entails both going to those far from Christ and His Church (evangelistic outreach) as well as nurturing the faith of newly-born believers and maturing the faith of long-time pilgrims (discipling endeavors). Congregations and ministries can best accomplish their Great Commission goals by envisioning, planning for and implementing; attractive outreaches that connect people to Jesus and His Church. This *Level #2 Philosophical-Principle* of *Evangelistic-Disciplemaking* is

informed and shaped by the *Level #1 Theological-Truths* of soteriology. It is from these Theological concepts and philosophical organizational principles then that *Level #3 Methodological-Models* emerge.

Gamesmanship

Gamesmanship is one of three philosophical approaches to competition and sport. It is partnered with sportsmanship and *Christmanship*. It describes a philosophy based on a secularized-pragmatic-ethic of engagement in and with sport. Its highest value is to win; regardless of how. As compared with sportsmanship that is based upon an ethic rooted in the humanistic-relativism of playing fair etc.; and *Christmanship* that espouses engaging in sport for the glory of God and in ways that honors all co-competitors; gamesmanship only prizes winning.

Internal Motivational Influences of Competition (IMIC)

IMIC—describes the pressures of competing because of, or against, internal forces such as one's pride, a personal level of excellence, goal, or a personal unmet ego need.

Leading-with-Buildings

Leading-with-Buildings is a *Level #2 Philosophical-Principle* that emphasizes the "build it and they will come" philosophy for SR&F Outreach Ministry. This philosophy has some merit and should not be unduly dismissed. High quality athletic and fitness facilities and equipment do attract those far from Jesus and His Church. However, such facilities by themselves are not enough. They must be missionally-programmed by leaders who envision, plan for and expedite *Redemptive-Repetitive-Relational* opportunities for church members to initiate and deepen relationships with friends, family members and associates for the purpose of *Evangelistic-Disciplemaking*. This phrase is often partnered with its corollary: *Building-with-Leaders*.

Level #1: Theological-Truths

This *Level #1* foundation for the *3-Tier Paradigm*, both informs and gives shape to *Level #2 Philosophical-Principles*; out which emerge *Level #3 Methodological-Models*. These truths form how SR&F Outreach Ministers think and what they believe. They are the foundation for why such ministries exist (*Evangelistic-Disciplemaking*) and how (Core Values) they conduct and operate their outreaches. Key words: think, believe and envision.

Level #2: Philosophical-Principles

This second level of the *3-Tier Paradigm* provides the organizational structure for SR&F Outreach Ministries. It is shaped and informed by *Level #1 Theological-Truths*; and is what *Level #3 Methodological-Models* emerge from. This organizational structure defines the when, where & with whom SR&F Outreach Ministries envision, plan for and administrate their outreaches. Key words: organize and administrate.

Level #3: Methodological-Models

This third level of the *3-Tier Paradigm* emerges out of the *Level #2 Philosophical-Principles* that provide the organizational structure for SR&F Outreach Ministries. Once a SR&F Outreach Ministry understands the when, where & with whom of their SR&F Outreach Ministries are to reach, they can then organize, administrate and implement their outreaches. Key words: do and act.

Mega-Event

Mega-Event is the term used at one end of the fourth of the *7- Continuums of Sports Outreach*. It describes one of *The Sports Outreach Community*'s *Methodological-Models*. This model uses large and exciting one-time events or activities to both attract those far from Christ and His Church and also to provide a *Platform-Proclamation* for the Gospel to be verbally proclaimed to a large group of people. *Mega-Event* is juxta-positioned with *Repetitive-Redemptive-Relational* on the fourth continuum.

Missional Programming

As distinguished from programming, the distinctive of Missional Programming has to do with programming with a clear Gospel-centered end-goal. Running a youth basketball league describes a church program. Facilitating a mission to youth through the strategy of a basketball ministry focuses congregational-based coaches on the Gospel-centered end-goal of *Evangelistic-Disciplemaking*.

Muscular Christian Era

The forerunner of The Sports Outreach Movement, Muscular Christianity was the term given to describe a particular philosophy that emerged in the early 1800's from Thomas Arnold's Rugby school and George Williams YMCA. It then flourished through the life and ministries of men like Moody, Mott, Naismith, Stagg and the Studd brothers. It culminated in the first few decades of the 1900's when Olympian Eric Liddell inspired the world by both his running to Gold in the 1924 Paris Olympics; but even more so, when he chose not to run on the Lord's Day and thus forfeited at least three other medals. The essence of Muscular

Christianity had to do with the integration of faith and sport. It devolved over the decades into more of a cultural ethos rather than a Christ-centered missional community.

Ologies

Short hand for the *Level #1 Theological-Truths* of the *3-Tier Paradigm* that inform and shape *Level #2 Philosophical-Principles*. The key and foundational *Ologies* include: ecclesiology; missiology; soteriology; cosmology; anthropology; and Christology.

Orthodoxy

Orthodoxy (not italicized because this is a common Theological term) refers to the necessity of establishing Theological and doctrinal foundations in general; and in specific it serves to undergird the *Ologies* of Sports Outreach that provide the basis for all *Level #1 Theological-Truths*.

Orthopraxy

Orthopraxy (not italicized because this is a common Theological term) refers to the necessity of establishing Biblically-based philosophies from which pragmatic methodologies can emerge. Orthopraxy has to do with the when, where & with whom of the 2nd level; the what of the 3rd level; and the how of the core values of the *3-Tier Paradigm*. In SR&F Outreach Ministry, a well envisioned orthopraxy will ensure the successful accomplishing of the *4-Fold Evaluative Rubric* that consists of being Strategically-Relevant and *Efficiently-Effective*.

Personality-over-Presence

Personality-over-Presence defines a *Level #3 Methodological-Model* based on a *Level #2 Philosophical-Principle* that organizes SR&F Outreaches for the purposes of having a "sports personality" give a verbal *Platform-Proclamation* of their faith, rather than envisioning, planning for and expediting outreaches based on creating on-going *Redemptive-Repetitive-Relational* activities that are focused on empowering local church missionaries to have an ever-growing and deepening presence in the lives of those far from Jesus and His Church.

Platform-Proclamation

The word platform is used in reference to a place from which to proclaim the Gospel. Proclamation refers to the verbal proclamation of the Gospel that takes place from various platforms. Such proclamations are almost exclusively delivered to large groups via mass-media. *Platform-Proclamation* is a *Level #3 Methodological-Model* that is most usually associated with Mega-Event-based outreaches. It utilizes the "platforms" associated with the notoriety afforded to elite athletes and coaches; so they can verbally "proclaim" their faith to the masses.

Proclamation-Affirmation

Proclamation-Affirmation (not italicized because this concept was coined by Jim Peterson) is the *Level #2 Philosophical-Principle* that is shaped and formed by *Level #1 Ologies* such as soteriology (Theology of salvation); missiology (Theology of missions); and ecclesiology (Theology of the Church). These *Ologies* suggest the most *Strategically-Relevant* and *Efficiently-Effective* outreaches are those based in *Repetitive-Redemptive-Relational* SR&F Outreaches. Such outreaches are created to attract those far from Christ and His Church to participate in activities (*Belong* – the first of *The 5-B's Process of Sports Outreach*) in which the Gospel is proclaimed through the organization and implementation of quality missional programming; as well as the Christ-like lives of congregational leaders and members. It is hoped these efforts and relationships result in opportunities for congregational members to "affirm" their faith verbally in ways that will encourage non-Christians to *Believe* (the second of *The 5-B's Process of Sports Outreach*) in Jesus; accepting as their Lord and Savior.

Progressive Intensity Levels of Competition (PIL's)

PIL is used to describe a concept concerning an ascending progression of seven distinct competitive levels within the volatility scale. Each level brings an increasing amount of intensity to the competition, and this increasing intensity carries with it an inherent potential exasperation for all involved.

Producing-Reproducing-Reproducers

This phrase summarizes the hope and end-goal of all SR&F Outreach Ministries. This hope is based in the Evangelistic-Disciplemaking transferable concept, and summarizes the end result of reaching those far from Christ and His Church with the Gospel: Dedicated-Disciples of Christ who reach others.

Redemption

One of four classical responses and reactions embraced by sport-related individuals who encounter the dilemma of integrating faith and their sport. It describes those who choose faith over sport by attempting to redeem individual sports-people (bring them to faith in Jesus) and also by attempting to redeem (adapt and alter the way sport is organized and participated in) the culture of sport.

Re-energizing

Re-energizing is the third part of the 3-I continuum for fully equipping SR&F Outreach ministers for the purpose of empowering them to envision, plan for, organize, administrate and evaluate a truly *Strategically-Relevant & Efficiently-Effective, Evangelistic-Disciplemaking* Sports Outreach Ministry. It defines the efforts to infuse SR&F Outreach ministers with new motivations and inspirations for reaching those far from Jesus and His Church. It also has to do with developing ongoing, personal, mentoring, relationships that enables SR&F Outreach ministers to become fully equipped for successful Great Commission endeavors.

Repetitive-Redemptive-Relational

Repetitive-Redemptive-Relational is found at one end of the fourth of the *7- Continuums* of Sports Outreach. It describes one expression of The Sports Outreach Movement's *Evangelistic-Disciplemaking, Philosophical-Principles.* This model uses repetitive and ongoing SR&F leagues, classes or activities to attract those far from Christ and His Church; and also to create interpersonal, relational *Evangelistic-Environments* for the Gospel to be experienced over a multiple-year, time frame. Based on Peterson's "Proclamation-Affirmation" concept; *Repetitive-Redemptive-Relational* verbal "affirmation" of the Gospel follows long periods of lived out "proclamation." Contrasted to a *Mega-Event* philosophy of gathering a large group of people to large scale event, *Repetitive-Redemptive-Relational* focuses on empowering and enabling, long-term, one-on-one or small group *Evangelistic-Disciplemaking* endeavors.

Rejection

One of four classical responses and reactions embraced by sport-related individuals who encounter the dilemma of integrating faith and their sport. It describes those who choose to leave sport because they cannot reconcile the demands of both. *Rejection* often means totally leaving sport but it can also describe a person who continues to engage in sport but rejects a specific aspect of it such as refusing to cheat; follow the instruction of a coach to purposely injure a fellow competitor or take harmful and illegal performance-enhancing substances.

Re-sourcing

Re-sourcing is the first part of the 3-I continuum for fully equipping SR&F Outreach Ministers for the purpose of empowering them to envision, plan for, organize, administrate and evaluate a truly *Strategically-Relevant & Efficiently-Effective, Evangelistic-Disciplemaking* Sports Outreach Ministry. It has to do with the creation, production and distribution of Re-sources that are: Christo-centric *Level #1 Theological-Truths*; Biblically-Based Level #2 *Philosophical-Principles*; and *Level #3 Methodological-Models*.

Re-training

Re-training is the second part of the *3-I* continuum for fully equipping SR&F Outreach ministers for the purpose of empowering them to envision, plan for, organize, administrate and evaluate a truly *Strategically-Relevant & Efficiently-Effective, Evangelistic-Disciplemaking* Sports Outreach Ministry. It has to do with Instructing SR&F Outreach ministers in how to most effectively utilize and employ the *Re-sources* that have been created, produced and distributed.

Singular-Commitment-Cost

The phrase *Singular-Commitment-Cost* is used in reference to ministries engaging in *Evangelistic-Disciplemaking* outreaches that emphasize there is a cost to becoming a disciple of Jesus. In comparison to Bonhoeffer's "Cheap Grace," churches, ministries and evangelists are encouraged to call people far from Jesus to become life-long, *Dedicated-Disciples*. Rather than simply asking people to "convert" *(Counting-Conversions)* by making a *Day's-Decision*, it is recommended all outreaches clearly communicate becoming a disciple of Jesus costs something! It includes not only receiving Jesus as Savior, but more so, making Him Lord of every area of their life. The *Singular-Commitment-Cost* describes the commitment churches and ministries need to make in "Changing-From" ministry models that strive to be winsome at the expense of proclaiming the whole Gospel; to "Changing-To" outreaches that present the Gospel in its entirety. It also describes the commitment a person needs to consider in making a decision to become a disciple.

Sportsmanship

Sportsmanship is one of three philosophical approaches to competition and sport. It describes an ethic based on the humanistic-relativism of playing fair; being a good teammate; and obeying the rules of the game. As compared with gamesmanship; a philosophy which highest value is to win, regardless of how; and *Christmanship* that espouses engaging in sport for the glory of God and in ways that honors all co-competitors; sportsmanship values ethics that are based in humanistic-relativism and therefore change according to a shifting societal culture.

Sports Outreach Community

• The phrase that generically describes the unique group within the Church of

Jesus Christ that uses SR&F Outreach Ministry to reach all who are far from Christ and His Church. It has four distinct expressions within local churches: a) congregational-based outreaches; b) sports-related para-ministries; c) fitness/wellness/wholeness based outreaches; and d) recreational/camping experiences and outreaches.
- This community also includes various sports-related, para-ministry models.
- The phrase *Sports Outreach Community* is preferred over Sports Outreach Movement because the former better communicates this group expresses itself within the Church, whereas Sports Outreach Movement connotes the efforts and activities occur as a separate movement from the Church.

Sports Outreach Movement
The phrase that describes the growing community within the Church of Jesus Christ using SR&F methodologies to reach all who are far from Christ and His Church. It has four distinct expressions: a) Congregational-based outreaches; b) sports-related para-ministries; c) fitness/wellness/wholeness based outreaches; and d) recreational/camping experiences and outreaches.

Sports-related, para-ministry
Based on the *Level #1 Ology* of ecclesiology (the Theology of the Church), the terminology para-ministry is preferred over para-church. It may seem a distinction without a difference and yet this seemingly subtle distinction can have significant and long-lasting negative implications. The word para means beside, and thus outside of. When used in relationship to the Church it communicates being outside of and thus, not part of the universal Church of Jesus. Conversely, para-ministry indicates a ministry that is outside of and yet beside the Church. There are congregational (often called local church) ministries and there are also ministries not based in congregations.

Sportianity
Sportianity (not italicized because it was not original with the author) is used to describe the thoughts, emotions and commitments of people who embrace one end of the Sportianity-Christianity Continuum. In essence its context describes people who make sport their highest priority and thus their commitment to, and their involvement in, sport becomes a type of religion.

Strategically-Relevant
Paired with *Efficiently-Effective*, it is the first half of the *4-Fold Evaluative Rubric*. *Strategically-Relevant* suggests the guideline congregations can use to help assess and determine whether or not a local church SR&F Outreach Ministry is actually

accomplishing its goal of engaging those whom are far from Christ and His Church. It is designed to aid local congregations to define and describe the most strategic and relevant sports, recreational activities and fitness initiatives within specific regions, countries and cultures of the world.

Success-Statistics

Success-Statistics is a phrase that describes how individual evangelists, churches, ministries and missions determine their effectiveness. Some count the number of people who make a *Day's-Decision* as indicated by the raising of their hand, praying a prayer or filling out a card (*Counting-Conversions*) to determine if their outreach was successful. Others see such *Days-Decisions* as but the first step in becoming life-long, *Dedicated-Disciples* and thus their effectiveness is only assessed by the number of people they have labored to "make disciples" of.

The Movement / The Sports Outreach Movement/The Local Church SR&F Movement

To move is to change location and position. A movement then has to do with change, repositioning and going somewhere—hopefully towards a destination. In this series of books there are two terms that are used interchangeably (The Sports Outreach Movement / The Movement) and a third that is very similar (The Local Church SR&F Movement). They can all be used to generally describe the activities of a like-minded group of people who are engaged in Christocentric ministry that is based in sport, recreation, fitness/wholeness/wellness and camping/outdoor pursuits. This Movement is generally agreed to have started in the 1940's when a number of activities occurred, beginning with the Venture for Victory initiating its international short-term sports mission trips and ministries such as the Billy Graham Associates began to use elite athletes and coaches as spokespersons at their crusades and events. It has morphed and expanded both in breadth and depth over the last decades. The phrase The Movement or The Sports Outreach Movement is used to describe and include all four quadrants, whereas The Local Church SR&F Movement is used to distinguish such activities within the confines of congregational outreach.

Volatility Scale

The Volatility Scale is an instrument that has been designed to chart and predict a competitor's experience. By combining the *EMIC*, *IMIC* and the *PIL's* it produces a measureable evaluative tool that analyzes what athletes, coaches and others will experience in a particular competitive event. *The Volatility Scale* contains four separate quadrants: *Enjoyment*; *Encounter*; *Explosion*; *Exasperation*.

Why; When-Where-With Whom; What

These are all tied to the *3-Tier Paradigm* and are specifically tied to one of the three levels of the paradigm:

• *Why*—is connected with the Christo-Centric *Level #1 Theological-Truths* which provide the basic rationale, ethical foundations for, The Sports Outreach Community

• *When-Where-With Whom*—are connected to the Biblically-based *Level #2 Philosophical-Principles* which provide the organizational structure for *The Sports Outreach Community*

• *What*—is connected with the *Strategically-Relevant* and *Efficiently-Effective Level #3 Methodological-Models* and describes the specific activities of *The Sports Outreach Community*

Without Reach We Have No Revenue and Without Revenue We Have No Reach

This phrase coined by Greg English communicates the local church SR&F Outreach Minister must balance "counting beans with counting souls." Both the ministry/outreach and the financing of the ministry are important. The financing empowers and enables the ministry and yet the ministry inspires the giving of the finances. The SR&F Outreach Ministers responsibility is to ensure both occur.

Frequently Asked Questions Concerning Salvation

Have you ever stood by your car at the end of a game and seen one of your teammates coming across the field and approaching you with that look? As you throw your sports gear in the trunk (boot), you are hoping this is indeed the moment you have been praying for. Yes! Your mate has a question about the devotional thought you shared moments before with the entire team! You rejoice over this "small step" in the *Evangelistic-Disciplemaking* process, but the real question is, do you have the answer to your mate's most difficult question concerning salvation.

His question about salvation isn't the one the Philippian jailer asked of Paul ("What must I do to be saved").[1] It's something much more complex. So, do you have the answer? Even if you do, perhaps the more important question is, have you prepared your coaches, captains or other leaders (your local church missionaries) with the answers to such questions?

In the course of ministering and relating to various people, SR&F Outreach Ministers and all whom they equip for ministry are often sought out for counsel in spiritual or other matters. None are more important than: "What must I do to be saved and other questions about salvation."

What follows attempts to serve as a primer for some of the basic but complex questions that are inevitably asked concerning the topic of salvation (soteriology). However, in keeping with the overall goals of this book, what follows are not exhaustive responses to any of the questions that might "pop up" on a softball field or become a "sticky wicket" on the cricket pitch, but hopefully they will provide SR&F Outreach Ministers, and all whom they train, with a few initial and basic responses to difficult questions that may be asked.

The following four questions are the ones I have received most often over my 40+ years in Sports Outreach Ministry.

---

1   Acts 16.25-31.

1. Can I Lose My Salvation

So, one of your instructors arrived ready to lead your church's fitness class. They were totally prepared for the physical activity. The equipment and music were ready to go and they had even been blessed by God with a great devotional to share. They knew the support team had been praying for this class and today they felt a special anointing of the Holy Spirit upon the class.

Afterward, your instructor was engaged in conversation with a person who shared that they were troubled. They expressed that they were currently not experiencing the joy, fulfillment, peace or empowerment in their Christian life and their question stopped the instructor in their tracks: "Have I lost my salvation?" Wow! You had trained her to be fitness class instructor, not a Theologian. What is she to do? What can you do to better prepare her?

Suggestions for answering this question...

First of all, it is recommended you prepare your leadership team for these situations by assuring them that they can be confident that God will be with them in these situations, and that God's Spirit will speak through them.[2]

Second, make sure they know that in this situation it is most likely the person is seeking assurance and peace of mind; as even the question they ask gives every indication they have accepted Jesus as Lord and Savior. Therefore, rather than wading into a lengthy Theological diatribe, it would seem your fitness leader has been blessed with an opportunity to help reassure her friend of her salvation. To that end, the following diagnostic questions are offered to help determine how to respond.

---

2   Matthew 10.19f.

SCOREBOARD

Key Verses – Can I Lose My Salvation?

Philippians 1.6 *"And I am sure of this, that He Who began a good work in you will bring it to completion at the day of Jesus Christ. "*

Ephesians 2.4, 5 *"But God, being rich in mercy, because of the great love with which He loved us, even when we were dead in our trespasses, made us alive together with Christ—by grace you have been saved..."*

Ephesians 2.8-10 *"For by grace you have been saved through faith. And this is not your own doing; it is the gift of God, not a result of works, so that no one may boast. For we are His workmanship..."*

- "Have you ever asked Jesus to be your Lord and Savior?"
    - If not, then the follow up question is: "Why not do that right now?"
    - If so, then…
        - "Why is it you now feel like you might have lost your salvation?"

Typically their answer to the second question is one of the following. Either they've engaged in some sinful activity/attitude that has shaken their basic relationship with Christ; are grieving a death or other loss; encountering a significant hurdle in their life; or experiencing a personal set-back of some sort.

Depending on their answer to the questions, the response could include: Offering to share in a simple prayer with them; encouraging them to re-engage in spiritual disciplines; sharing relevant Bible verses (see scoreboard - Can I lose my salvation? on page 142); or perhaps in certain situations, referring them for professional counseling. It is important to remember listening communicates that the leader both loves and cares. This is perhaps the most important thing that can be done.

Third, be prepared with relevant Bible verses (See Key Verses Scoreboard on page 142) It is recommended all SR&F Outreach Leaders put these verses in a file on their cell phone for handy reference!

Finally, and most importantly, reassure the person that salvation is dependent on God; not a person. Of course, this assumes a person's conversion (salvation) is real and authentic.

One very important recommendation: Consult with your Lead Pastor and/or Elder Board!

This is a Theological question (often stated as "once saved, always saved") that has been debated through the millennia, and thus it is vitally important to talk with your Lead Pastor about your congregation's and denomination's position on this. It is imperative to be on the same page with your congregation's leadership on this and every Theological issue.

2. Do I Need to Get Baptized

Another question SR&F Outreach Ministers often are asked in relationship to salvation has to do with being baptized. This of course raises one of the more controversial Theological debates the Church has ever faced. In fact, the issue of baptism has been a major cause for the creation of a number of denominational splits.

Scripture is clear that baptism is not an absolute requirement for salvation but it is the expected norm for all disciples of Jesus. This can be seen in both the words and life of Jesus.

SCOREBOARD

Key Verses – Do I Need To Be Baptized?

Matthew 28:19, 20 *"Go ye therefore, and teach all nations, baptizing them in the name of the Father, and of the Son, and of the Holy Ghost: teaching them to observe all things whatsoever I have commanded you: and, lo, I am with you always, even unto the end of the world. Amen."*

Acts 2:38 *"Then Peter said unto them, 'Repent, and be baptized every one of you in the name of Jesus Christ for the remission of sins, and ye shall receive the gift of the Holy Ghost.' "*

Acts 16:31, 33 *"And they said, 'Believe on the Lord Jesus Christ, and thou shalt be saved, and thy house.' And he took them the same hour of the night, and washed their stripes; and was baptized, he and all his, straightway."*

Jesus personally sought out baptism,[3] and yet when he promised the thief on the cross eternal life He demonstrated baptism was not required for salvation and eternal life.[4] So, it follows that there is a major distinctive difference between baptism being required and it being the normative recommendation.

Relevance of Baptism for SR&F Outreach Ministry

Pertaining to baptism, the major relevance for SR&F Outreach Ministers and all the local church missionary leaders they train has to do with how baptism enhances and empowers the "making of disciples." Specifically, this third "*B*"[5] of Sports Outreach is a most important step in "making disciples" because it emphasizes making a public confession of faith.[6]

It's one thing to "raise a hand" at a league-ending evangelistic outreach event or even privately "pray the sinner's prayer" with a league director or coach; it's quite another to stand in front of a congregation and publically proclaim Jesus is your personal Lord and Savior. The main emphasis here is in the prioritizing of having new believers make a public proclamation of their faith; a most vital step

---

3   Matthew 3.13-17.
4   Luke 23.39-43.
5   Consult Chapter 9 of this book for a more in depth discussion of baptism.
6   Consult chapter 5 of my book *The Fundamentals of Sports Outreach* for a full explanation and understanding of the *"5B's"* of Sports Outreach and the relevance of baptism.

in the end goal of "making of disciples." What form the baptism takes is not as important, and differs between denominations both in timing (infant or adult) and in its mode (immersion/sprinkling/pouring/ or not using water).[7]

Suggestions for answering this question:

First, for this discussion the main point is not for the SR&F Leader to engage in a lengthy debate about the mode or timing of baptism, but rather about the strategic nature of having new followers of Jesus make a public declaration of faith. This is the most relevant aspect of answering the question about baptism that was raised by a participant in a fitness class or a player in a league.

Second, rather than waiting for someone to ask this question, it is highly recommended for SR&F Leaders to lovingly encourage all new Christians to make their conversion public by being baptized (or confirmed).

Third, SR&F Outreach Ministers and all the local church missionaries they train (league directors, coaches and class teachers, etc.) are encouraged to have "at the ready" the next steps for the new Christian that would include a plan for baptism (or confirmation).[8]

Fourth, again it is recommended to have the verses found in the Scoreboard "Key Verses—Do I need to be baptized" entered into a file on a cell phone for easy reference.

Finally, get the person registered for the church's class on baptism and get the date scheduled for the public baptism or confirmation.

3. Do Babies Who Die Go To Heaven?

There's a Celtic tradition of prayer that I've practiced for decades that has been a most helpful aide to keeping my prayer-life relevant, fresh and intercessory on behalf of those in need of comfort. This spiritual discipline entails praying for specific requests on specific days of the week that are naturally associated with that day of the week. For example, one of the things to pray for on Friday has to do with praying for parents who have lost a child. Why Fridays… because the Heavenly Father's Son died on a Friday. Unfortunately, this harsh reality has been experienced by myriads of suffering parents, and thus it should come as no surprise this question surfaces so often.

Suggestions for answering this question:

First, remember grieving parents, experience what is considered by many the greatest agony anyone can encounter on earth—the loss of a child. So while it should not come as a surprise that this is one of the first questions asked by new Christians who have suffered a miscarriage or who have had to bury an older child, it is vital to be very warmly sensitive to the deep wound in the person asking the question. It should not be surprising that SR&F local church missionaries

---

7   Quakers have a history of not using the outward sign of water, believing spiritual baptism to suffice.
8   Consult the next steps offered in the Scoreboard in Chapter 7 of this book entitled: Salvation Success.

SCOREBOARD

Key Verses – Do Babies Who Die Go To Heaven?

Matthew 19:13-15 *"Let the little children come to me, and do not hinder them, for to such belongs the kingdom of heaven.*

Luke 1.15 *"... for he will be great before the Lord....even from his mother's womb."*

Jeremiah 1.5 *"Before I formed you in the womb I knew you, and before you were born I consecrated you."*

2 Samuel 12:15.23 *"...I shall go to him, but he will not return to me."*

(coaches, league directors etc.) may well encounter such a question, and would be wise to be ready for this inquiry.

Second, when such a question is asked, the league director or team coach is encouraged to listen rather than talk as they will find this to be a perfect time to "live out the Gospel" ("weep with those who weep").[9] While it's certain that the person who asks this question will want to hear what is said, they will more so remember how they felt about this encounter. While words are heard, love is felt; and those feelings most often outlive, and communicate far deeper, than what is said.

Third, yet, though what is said remains crucial, keep in mind what is said will be well received if it is reassuring and comforting.

Fourth, once again it is recommended to have the key verses found in the Scoreboard "Key Verses, Do babies who die go to heaven?" (above) at the ready via a cell phone file. These concepts are best shared in a private conversation that is not rushed.

Fifth, ... and a box of Kleenex is recommended.

Important Concepts

An important concept to be shared is that a person is judged (condemned—as in not allowed into heaven) based on their willful, conscious rejection of God's love and will for their life.[10] This alone would suggest that not only the preborn and the infant, but also those who are mentally incapacitated, are incapable of willfully and consciously rejecting God.

---

9   Romans 12.15-18.
10   2 Corinthians 5.10; 1 Corinthians 6.9; Revelation 20.12

Further Explanations of Important Verses

Other scriptures that bring comfort include: a) David's statement about his infant son who died shortly after birth and tells that David looked forward to meeting the child in the afterlife; b) children being chosen in their mother's womb; and c) Jesus's own encounters with children. (See the Scoreboard on page 146)

The account of David grieving the loss of his infant son is profound in two ways. First, it clearly demonstrates the deep sorrow of a grieving father. Second, it communicates the foundational Christian belief that while the departed son cannot come back to his father, the father can see that child again in heaven!

In addition, there are passages that can encourage the hearts of grieving parents in the fact they teach that children were formed, chosen and consecrated in their mother's womb.[11] This teaches that death cannot "steal" a child from God.

Then of course, there is the most wonderful story related in the gospels that record Jesus's great love for the little children, and his claim that they belong to His kingdom.[12] All I can say is; Hallelujah, what a Savior!

All of this of course lines up with what the entire Bible teaches about God being a loving Father and that may well be the greatest source of comfort to grieving parents when lovingly and sensitively shared in the midst of a SR&F Outreach Ministry.[13]

4. What About Those Who Never Hear the Gospel

There is a poignant story about the famous Scottish missionary David Livingston and a tribal chief who had converted to Christianity under Livingston's ministry.

When the reality of the knowledge that the only way to heaven and eternal life comes through belief in Christ was fully understood by the tribal chief; he asked Livingston the following questions:

Question: There is no way to heaven without hearing about and believing in Jesus? **Answer:** hearing and believing in Christ is the only way.

Question: When did your ancestors know this Gospel truth about Jesus? **Answer:** 1,800 years ago.

Question: What took your ancestors so long to come and tell my ancestors about Jesus? **Answer:** Silence!

Reality Check: Before delving into this question, it is important to re-emphasize the significance of not only this subtopic and chapter but also this entire book. It boils down to: where someone will spend eternity! This is not just another esoteric Theological discussion for the "ivory tower" elite! What we

---

11   Luke 1.15; Jeremiah 1.5.

12   Matthew 19.13-15; Mark 10.13-16; Luke 18.15-17.

13   It must be pointed out that this is a somewhat controversial subject and that regardless of one's position or belief, a baby's eternal status is up to God. Nonetheless we can find comfort in trusting God with this. Once more it is recommended to discuss this with church leadership so as to be in sync with the broader church.

are dealing with here literally makes the difference between heaven and hell. I don't believe any of us would ever want someone to say to us: "Why did it take you so long to tell me this truth?!" May it never be said of us that our friends, family members, co-workers or those who play on our team in our church league or participate in the fitness class we teach at our church never heard the Gospel from us!

So, assuming we have proclaimed faith in Christ in our lives, and then affirmed our faith by verbally sharing the Gospel with a teammate, it just may be that our teammate will ask us about the person who has never heard the Gospel, and where they will spend eternity. How do we answer this question?

Suggestions for answering this question:

First, affirm and compliment the person for caring about the spiritual condition of those who have never come in contact with the Gospel.

Second, also confirm this is one of the more difficult Theological concepts that Christianity has to answer because it is not simply or directly addressed in the Bible. That doesn't mean however, that a Biblical answer can't be attained.

Third, the best answer is found in one of Paul's letters in a section on prayer where Paul is admonishing Timothy to pray for all people because He desires for "all people to be saved and to come to the knowledge of the truth."[14] So the main thing to communicate is that we can rest assured that God desires all people to come to Him.

A second Biblical concept to share, centers on Abraham. Abraham lived centuries before Jesus and thus had never heard about Christ and yet he was saved by faith.[15] This would lead us to believe that faith in God is what is important for all those who have never heard of Jesus. Now this may seem to open up the thought that all religions that teach faith in God result in salvation for those outside of Christianity.[16] Nothing could be farther from the truth. The truth about Abraham has to do with a loving God counting people who have faith in Him as righteous and justified; and thus, granting them salvation based on His mercy rather than something they did to earn salvation. So, God clearly saved many people before Jesus came to earth in human form but other questions arise such as: a) How were people saved before Jesus; b) how many people were saved; and c) in what way were they saved? These deeper questions necessitate a longer and more in depth study of soteriology.

Finally, this initial discussion may well provide the opportunity to invite the questioner to engage in a Bible study that could explore this and any other questions. It is recommended to all SR&F Leaders to see these kinds of inquiries

14   1 Timothy 2.4.
15   Romans 4.1-25.
16   This would be considered a certain version of the theory called Universalism, which teaches that all are saved and go to heaven. However, Universalism is a heretical (incorrect) distortion of Christian Theology.

as opportunities to fulfill the latter couple of aspects of the Great Commission: "teach" and "make disciples." Salvation is one of the most cherished beliefs of the Christian faith, one worthy of much attention and study. When such a question is asked, don't miss the opportunity to "teach" and thus, "make a disciple."

SCOREBOARD

Key Verses – What About Those Who Are Never Exposed To The Gospel

Romans 1:18-20 *"For the wrath of God is revealed...against all ungodliness and unrighteousness of men, who suppress the truth.... So they are without excuse."*

Matthew 19:13-15 *"Let the children come unto Me."*

Romans 4 - *The story of Abraham was justified by his faith. Other Verses About Salvation*

Ephesians 2.8f *"For by grace you have been saved through your faith. And this is not your own doing; it is the gift of God, not a result of works, so that no one may boast."*

Acts 4.12 *"And there is salvation in no one else, for there is no other name under heaven given among men by which we must be saved."*

John 3.16 *"For God so loved the world, that He gave His only Son, that whoever believes in Him should not perish but have eternal life."*

Titus 3.5-7 *"...He saved us, not because of works done by us in righteousness, but according to His own mercy, by the washing of regeneration and renewal of the Holy Spirit, whom He poured out on us richly through Jesus Christ our Savior, so that being justified by His grace we might become heirs according to the hope of eternal life."*

Sources Consulted For This Book

Babb, K. "Where College Football is a Religion and Religion Shapes College Football," *Washington Post*, 29 Aug. 2014. Available at <http://www.washingtonpost.com/sports/colleges/where-college-football-is-a-religion-and-religion-shapes-college-football/2014/08/29/8d03de32-2dfa-11e4-bb9b-997ae96fad33_story.html?wpmk=MK0000200>.

Bonhoeffer, Dietrich. *The Cost of Discipleship*. Revised [2nd] and unabridged ed., containing material not previous translated. New York: Macmillan, 1963, c1959.

Boyers, John. *Beyond the Final Whistle: A Life of Football and Faith*. London: Hodder and Stoughton, 2000.

Boyers, John. "Manchester United FC." *Being a Chaplain*, edited by Miranda Threlfall-Holmes and Mark Newitt. London: SPCK, 2011, pp. 81-84.

Brewster, Paul L. *Andrew Fuller: Model Pastor Theologian*. Nashville, TN: B&H Academic, 2010.

Chan, Francis. *Letters To The Church*. Colorado Springs, CO: David C. Cook, 2018.

Chawner, D. "A Reflection on the Practice of Sports Chaplaincy." *Urban Theology*, vol. 3, no. 1, 2009, pp. 75-80. Available at <http://www.urbantheology.org/journals/journal-3-1/a-reflection-on-the-practice-of-sports-chaplaincy>.

Deford, F. "Religion in Sport." *Sports Illustrated*, vol. 44, no. 16, 1976, pp. 88-100.

Esar, Evan, editor. *The Treasury of Humorous Quotations*. English edition edited by Nicolas Bentley. London: Phoenix House, 1951.

Gamble, Richard, Andrew Parker, and Denise M. Hill. "Football, Sports Chaplaincy and Sport Psychology: Connections and Possibilities." *Sports Chaplaincy: Trends, Issues and Debates,* edited by Andrew Parker, Nick J Watson, John B White. London: Routledge, 2016, pp. 182-194.

Heskins, Jeffery and Matt Baker, editors. *Footballing Lives: As Seen by Chaplains in the Beautiful Game.* Norwich [Eng.]: Canterbury Press, 2006

Hoffman, S.J. *Good Game: Christianity and the Culture of Sports*, Waco, TX: Baylor University Press, 2010.

Holm, N. "Toward a Theology of the Ministry of Presence in Chaplaincy," *Journal of Christian Education*, vol. 52, no. 1, 2009, pp. 7–22. Available at <http://www.academia.edu/1256854/Toward_a_Theology_of_the_Ministry_of_Presence_in_Chaplaincy>.

Linville, Greg. *Putting the Church Back in the Game: The Ecclesiology of Sports Outreach,* Canton, OH: Overwhelming Victory Press, 2019

_____. "Sports Chaplaincy and North American Society: Strategies for Winning in the Club House." In Parker, Andrew, Nick J. Watson, John B. White, editors. *Sports Chaplaincy: Trends, Issues, and Debates.* London: Routledge, 2016.

_____. *Sports Outreach Fundamentals: Biblically-Based, Philosophical-Principles for Strategically-Relevant & Efficiently-Effective Disciplemaking.* Canton, OH: Overwhelming Victory Press, 2018.

Lloyd-Jones, David Martyn. *Darkness and Light: An Exposition of Ephesians 4:17-5:17.* Grand Rapid, MI: Baker Book House, 1982.

McDowell, Josh. *Evidence That Demands a Verdict: Historical Evidence for the Christian Scriptures.* 2nd ed. San Bernardino CA: Here's Life Publishers, 1981.

_____. *More Evidence That Demands a Verdict: Historical Evidences for Christian Scriptures.* Rev. ed. San Bernardino, CA: Here's Life Publishers, 1981.

Murray, Andrew. *Absolute Surrender.* Chicago: Fleming H. Revell, 1897.

Parker, Andrew, Nick J. Watson, John B. White, editors. *Sports Chaplaincy: Trends, Issues, and Debates.* London: Routledge, 2016.

Rainer, Thom S. and Eric Geiger. *Simple Church: Returning to God's Process for Making Disciples.* Nashville: B&H Publishing Group, 2011.

Rushworth-Smith, David. *Off the Ball: a Sports Chaplain at Work.* Basingstoke [Eng.]: Marshalls, 1985.

Stetzer, Ed. *Christians in the Age of Outrage: How to Bring Our Best When the World Is at Its Worst.* Carol Stream, IL: Tyndale House Publishers, 2018. ISBN 978-1-4964-3362-6

Threlfall-Holms, Miranda and Mark Newitt. *Being a Chaplain.* London: SPCK, 2011. (SPCK Library of Ministry)

Walker, Jon. *Costly Grace 90-Day Devotional: a Contemporary View of Bonhoeffer's The Cost of Discipleship.* Abilene, TX: Leafwood Publishers, 2010.

Wood, Stuart. *Keeping Faith in the Team: The Chaplain's Story.* London: Longman Dartman and Todd, 2011

Sources Consulted For This Book Series

Personal letters and correspondence

Decades of listening to Renewing Your Mind by Ligonier and Truth for Life broadcasts

Akabusi, Kriss and Stuart Weir. *Wisdom for the Race of Life*. Oxford: Bible Reading Fellowship, 1999.

Aldrich, Joseph C. *Life-Style Evangelism: Learning to Open Your Life to Those Around You*. Portland, OR: Multnomah Press, 1993.

Anderson, J. Kerby. *Christian Ethics in Plain Language*. Nashville, TN: Thomas Nelson, 2005.

Atcheson, Wayne. *Impact for Christ: How FCA Has Influenced the Sports World*. Grand Island, NE: Cross Training Publ., 1994. About the Fellowship of Christian Athletes.

Baker, William J. *Playing with God: Religion and Modern Sport*. Cambridge, MA: Harvard University Press, 2007.

Barton, Bruce. *The Man Nobody Knows*. New York: Collier Books, 1987, c1925.

Bateman, Charles T. *The Life of General Booth*. New York: Association Press, 1912.

Begg, Alastair. *Pathway to Freedom*. Sound recording (12 CDs). Cleveland, OH: Truth for Life, 2003. ID 20501. Series of sermons on Exodus 20, the Ten Commandments.

Beisser, Arnold R. *Madness in Sports*. New York: Appleton-Century Crofts, 1977. Quoted in The Plain Dealer, section G, Jan. 18, 1987, p. 3.

Belcher, Richard and Richard P. Belcher, Jr. *A Layman's Guide to the Sabbath Question*. Southbridge, MA: Crowne Publications, 1991.

Benge, Janet and Geoff Benge. *Eric Liddell: Something Greater Than Gold*. Seattle, WA: YWAM Publishers, 1998.

Bonhoeffer, Dietrich. *The Cost of Discipleship*. Revised [2nd] and unabridged ed., containing material not previous translated. New York: Macmillan, 1963, c1959.

Braisted, Ruth Evelyn Wilder. *In This Generation: The Story of Robert P. Wilder*. New York: Published for the Student Volunteer Movement by Friendship Press, 1941.

Brewster, Paul. *Andrew Fuller: Model Pastor-Theologian*. Nashville, TN; B&H Publishing Group, 2010.

Broneer, Oscar. *The Odeum*. Cambridge, MA: Published for the American School of Classical Studies at Athens by Harvard University Press, 1932. (American School of Classical Studies at Athens. Corinth; v. 10)

_____. *The South Stoa and Its Roman Successors*. Princeton, NJ: American School of Classical Studies at Athens, 1954. (Corinth; v. 1, pt. 4)

_____. *Temple of Poseidon*. Princeton, NJ: American School of Classical Studies at Athens, 1971. (Isthmia; v. 1)

Browne, Leonard. *Sport and Recreation, and Evangelism in the Local Church*. Bramcote, Nottingham, Eng.: Grove Books, 1991.

Buchanan, Mark. *The Rest of God: Restoring Your Soul by Restoring the Sabbath*. Nashville, TN: Thomas Nelson, 2006.

Byl, John. *Intramural Recreation: A Step-By-Step Guide to Creating an Effective Program*. Champaign, IL: Human Kinetics, 2002.

_____. *Organizing Successful Tournaments*. Champaign, IL: Human Knetics, 1999.

Byl, John and Tom Visker. *Physical Education, Sports and Wellness: Looking to God As We Look at Ourselves*. Sioux City, IA: Dordt Press, 1999.

Chariots of Fire (Videorecording) / Warner Bros. Pictures; a Warner Bros. and Ladd Company release; presented by Allied Stars; an Enigma production; original screenplay by Colin Welland; produced by David Puttnam; directed by Hugh Hudson. Burbank, CA: Warner Home

Video, 2003. DVD. Originally produced as a British motion picture in 1981.

Church Sports International (a ministry partner under Share the Savior organization (website): www.sharethesavior.org

Clowney, Edmund, P. *The Church*. Downers Grove, IL: Inter Varsity Press, 1995.

Coakley, Jay J. *Sports in Society: Issues and Controversies*. 9th ed. Boston: McGraw Hill Higher Education, 2007.

Conner, Ray. *The Ministry of Recreation*. Nashville, TN: Convention Press, 1992.

Connor, Steve. *A Sporting Guide to Eternity: A Devotional for Competitive People*. Fearn, Eng.: Christian Focus, 2002.

_____. *Sports Outreach: Principles + Practice for Successful Sports Ministry*. Ross-shire, Scotland: Christian Focus Publications, 2003.

Conrad, Tim. *Game Plan*. Florissant, CO: Thistle Productions, 2009. (Sapphire Lake series)

_____. *Go the Distance*. Florissant, CO: Thistle Productions, 2010. (Sapphire Lake series)

Couey, Richard B. *Building God's Temple*. Minneapolis: Burgess Pub. Co., 1982.

CSRM: The Association of Church Sports and Ministers (website): www.csrm.org

Dahl, Gordon. *Work, Play and Worship: In a Leisure-Oriented Society*. Minneapolis: Augsburg Pub. House, 1972.

Daniels, Graham and Stuart Weir. *Born to Play!* Bicester, Eng.: Frampton House, 2004.

_____. *The Sports Stadium: How to Share Your Faith in the World of Sport*. Bicester, Eng.: Frampton House Publications, 2005.

Darden, Robert. *Into the End Zone*. Nashville, TN: Thomas Nelson, 1989.

Davis, John Jefferson. *Evangelical Ethics: Issues Facing the Church Today.* 3rd ed., rev. and expanded. Phillipsburg, NJ: P&R Pub., 2004.

Dickson, John. *The Best Kept Secret of Christian Mission: Promoting the Gospel with More Than Our Lips.* Grand Rapids, MI: Zondervan, 2010.

Digby, Andrew Wingfield and Stuart Weir. *Winning is Not Enough: Sports Stars Who Are Going for Gold and For God.* London: Marshall Pickering, 1991.

Doggett, Lawrence Locke. *The Life of Robert R. McBurney.* Cleveland: F.M. Barton, 1902.

Dorsett, Lyle W. *A Passion for Souls: The Life of D.L. Moody.* Chicago: Moody Press, 1997.

Driscoll, Mark. *The Radical Reformission: Reaching Out without Selling Out.* Grand Rapids, MI: Zondervan, 2004.

Ehrmann, Joe. *Inside Out Coaching: How Sports Can Transform Lives.* New York: Simon & Schuster, 2011.

Eisenman, Tom. *Every Day Evangelism: Making the Most of Life's Common Moments.* Downers Grove, IL: InterVarsity Press, 1987.

The English Standard Version Bible: Containing the Old and New Testaments with Apocrypha. New York: Oxford University Press, 2009.

Evans, Tony, Jonathan Evans and Dillon Burroughs. *Get in the Game.* Chicago: Moody Publishers, 2006.

Finney, Charles G. *How to Promote a Revival.* Antrim, Ireland: Revival Pub. Co., 1948.

Gardiner, E. Norman. *Athletics of the Ancient World.* Oxford, Eng.: Clarendon Press, 1930.

Garner, John, ed. *Recreation and Sports Ministry: Impacting the Postmodern Culture.* 2nd ed. Lynchburg, VA: Liberty University Press, 2017.

Gough, Russell Wayne. *Character is Everything: Promoting Ethical Excellence in Sport.* Fort Worth, TX: Harcourt Brace College Publishers, 1997.

Green, Michael. *Evangelism Through the Local Church.* Nashville, TN: Oliver-Nelson, 1992.

Grubb, Norman P. *C.T. Studd, Athlete and Pioneer.* Atlantic City, NJ: World-Wide Revival Prayer Movement, 1947.

Guttman, Allen. *Sport Spectators.* New York: Columbia University Press, 1986.

Hamilton, Duncan. *For The Glory: The Untold and Inspiring Story of Eric Liddell, Hero of Chariots of Fire.* New York, NY: Penguin Press, 2016.

Harris, Harold Arthur. *Greek Athletes and Athletics.* Bloomington: Indiana University Press, 1966, c1964.

————. *Sport in Greece and Rome.* Ithaca, NY: Cornell University Press, 1989. Originally published 1972.

Heschel, Abraham Joshua. *The Sabbath: Its Meaning for Modern Man.* New York: Farrar, Straus & Giroux, 2005, c1951.

Higgs, Robert. *God in the Stadium: Sports and Religion in America.* Lexington, KY: University Press of Kentucky, 1995.

Hodder-Williams, J. E. *The Life of Sir George Williams: Founder of the Young Men's Christian Association.* New York: A.C. Armstrong, 1906.

Hoffman, Shirl James. *Good Game: Christianity and the Culture of Sports.* Waco, TX: Baylor University Press, 2010.

Hoffman, Shirl James, ed. *Sport and Religion.* Champaign, IL: Human Kinetics Books, 1992.

Holy Bible, Containing the Old and New Testaments: Authorized King James Version, With a New System of Connected References ... New York: Oxford University Press, 1945. Originally published 1611, the most published English Bible, available in countless editions.

The Holy Bible: New Century Version, Containing the Old and New Testaments. Dallas, TX: Word Bibles, c1991.

The Holy Bible: New International Version, Containing the Old Testament and the New Testament. Grand Rapids, MI: Zondervan Bible Publishers, c1978.

Hopkins, Charles Howard. *History of the Y.M.C.A. in North America.* New York: Association Press, 1951.

Hughes, Thomas, 1822-1896. *The Manliness of Christ.* Philadelphia: H. Altemus, 1896.

_____. *Tom Brown at Oxford.* First published: Cambridge, Eng.: Macmillan, 1861. Many modern editions are available.

_____. *Tom Brown's School Days.* First published: Cambridge, Eng.: Macmillan, 1857.
Many modern editions are available.

Hunter, George G. *How to Reach Secular People.* Nashville, TN: Abingdon Press, 1992.

Johnson, Elliot. *Focus on the Finish Line: Hurdles Female Athletes Face in the Race of Life.* Grand Island, NE: Cross Training Pub., 1997.

_____. *Heroes of the Faith: Advice from God's Athletes.* Grand Island, NE: Cross Training Pub., 1995.

_____. *The Point After: Advice from God's Athletes.* Grand Rapids, MI: Zondervan, 1987.

_____. *Strong to the Finish.* Grand Island, NE: Cross Training Pub., 1998.

Johnson, Elliot and Al Schierbaum. *Up Close with The Savior.* Grand Island, NE: Cross Training Pub., 1994.

Keddie, John W. and Sebastian Coe. *Running the Race: Eric Liddell, Olympic Champion.* New York: Evangelical Press, 2007.

Kluck, Ted. *The Reason for Sport: A Christian Fanifesto.* Chicago: Moody Press, 2009.

Kohn, Alfie. *No Contest: The Case Against Competition.* Boston: Houghton Mifflin, 1986.

Krattenmaker, Tom. *Onward Christian Athletes: Turning Ballparks into Pulpits and Players into Preachers.* Lanham, MD: Rowman & Littlefield, 2010.

Ladd, Tony and James A. Mattheson. *Muscular Christianity: Evangelical Protestants and the Development of American Sport.* Grand Rapids, MI: Baker Books, 1999.

Larson, Knute. *The Great Human Race: How to Endure in the Marathon of Life.* Akron, OH: The Chapel Press, 2002.

Linville, Greg. *A Contemporary Christian Ethic of Competition.* Canton, OH: First Friends Church, [1990s?]

_____. *Christmanship: A Theology of Competition and Sport.* Canton, OH: Oliver House Publishing Inc., 2014.

_____. *Does Sport Ministry Aid Local Church Evangelism?* Ashland, OH: Ashland Theological Seminary, 2007. Thesis (D. Min.)—Ashland Theological Seminary.

_____. *Executive Director's Blog.* www.csrm.org/blog.html Accessed 8 April 2013.
This blog contains many of Greg Linville's writings.

_____. *Overwhelming Victory: A Coaching Manual.* Ashland, OH: Ashland Theological Seminary, 1987. Project (M.A.)—Ashland Theological Seminary.

_____. *Putting the Church Back in the Game: The Ecclesiology of Sports Outreach,* Canton, OH: Overwhelming Victory Press, 2019

_____. *Sports Outreach Fundamentals: Biblically-Based, Philosophical-Principles for Strategically-Relevant & Efficiently-Effective Disciplemaking.* Canton, OH: Overwhelming Victory Press, 2018.

_____. *Surrounded by Witnesses*. Canton, OH: Association Press, 2005.

_____. *Theology of Competition*. Canton, OH: Overwhelming Victory Ministries, [1990s].

Magnusson, Sally. *The Flying Scotsman*. New York: Quartet Books, 1981. Biography of Eric Liddell.

Malony, Newton and Southard, Samuel, eds. *Handbook of Religious Conversion*. Birmingaham, AL: Religious Education Press, 1992.

Martens, Rainier. *Joy and Sadness in Children's Sports*. Champaign, IL: Human Kinetics Press, 1978.

Mason, Bryan. *Beyond the Gold: What Every Church Needs to Know About Sports Ministry*. Milton Keynes, Eng.: Authentic Media Ltd., 2011.

_____. *Into the Stadium: An Active Guide to Sport and Recreation Ministry in the Local*
Church. Milton Keynes, Eng.: Authentic Media Ltd., 2003.

Mattingly, Don. *Recreation for Youth*. Nashville, TN: Convention Press, 1986.

McCasland, David. *Eric Liddell: Pure Gold: A New Biography of the Olympic Champion Who Inspired Chariots of Fire*. Grand Rapids, MI: Discovery House, 2001.

McCown, Lowrie and Valirie J. Gin. *Focus on Sport in Ministry*. Marietta, GA: 360° Sports, 2003.

McLemore, Clinton W. *Street Smart Ethics: Succeeding in Business Without Selling Your Soul*. Louisville, KY: Westminster John Know Press, 2003.

Michener, James A. *Sports in America*. New York: Random House, 1976.

Moore, R. Laurence (Robert Laurence). *Touchdown Jesus: The Mixing of Sacred and Secular in American History*. Louisville, KY: Westminster John Knox Press, 2003.

Morrow, Greg and Steve Morrow. *Recreation: Reaching Out, Reaching In, Reaching Up*. Nashville, TN: Convention Press, 1986.

Morse, Richard Cary, 1841-1926. *History of the North American Young Men's Christian Associations*. New York: Association Press, 1913.

_____. *My Life with Young Men: Fifty Years in the Young Men's Christian Association*. New York: Association Press, 1918.

Murray, Iain H. *A Scottish Christian Heritage*. Edinburgh: The Banner of Truth Trust, 2006.

Neal, Wes. *The Handbook on Athletic Perfection*. 3rd ed. Grand Island, NE: Cross Training Publishing, 1981.

Neal, Wes. *The Handbook on Coaching Perfection*. 2nd ed. Milford, MI: Mott Media, 1981.

Newman, Wendell T. *Organizing for Recreation Ministry*. Nashville, TN: Convention Press, 1990.

Nix, Stan. *Sports Stories and the Bible*. Carlsbad, CA: Magnus Press, 2003.

Olivova, Vera. *Sport and Games in the Ancient World*. New York: St. Martin's Press, 1985.

Oswald, Rodger. *Sports Ministry and the Church: A Philosophy of Ministry*. Campbell, CA: Church Sports International, 1990s.

_____. *A Theology of Sports Ministry*. Campbell, CA: Church Sports International, 1993.

Parker, Andrew, Watson, Nick J. and White John B., eds. *Sports Chaplaincy: Trends, Issues and Debates*. New York, NY: Routledge, 2016.

Parrott, Mike. *Team Huddles: Sports Devotionals*. Grand Island, NE: Cross Training Pub., 2000.

Peterson, Jim. *Church Without Walls*. Colorado Springs, CO: Nav Press, 1991.

_____. *Living Proof.* Grand Rapids, MI: Zondervan, 1997.

Piggin, Stuart and John Roxborough. *The St. Andrew Seven: The Finest Flowering of Missionary Zeal in Scottish History.* Edinburgh; Carlisle, PA: Banner of Truth Trust, 1985.

Pollock, John Charles. *The Cambridge Seven: A Call to Christian Service.* London: Inter-Varsity Press, 1969, c1955.

Prebish, Charles S. *Religion and Sport: The Meeting of Sacred and Profane.* Westport, CN: Greenwood Press, 1993.

Prime, Derek. *Active Evangelism: Putting the Evangelism of Acts into Practice.* Ross-shire, Scotland: Christian Focus, 2003.

Putney, Clifford. *Muscular Christianity, Manhood and Sports in Protestant America, 1880-1920.* Cambridge, MA: Harvard University Press, 2001.

Rader, Benjamin G. *American Sports: From the Age of Folk Games to the Age of Televised Sports.* Englewood Cliffs, NJ: Prentice Hall, 1990.

Rainer, Thom S. and Lewis A. Drummond, eds. *Evangelism in the Twenty-First Century: The Critical Issues.* Wheaton, IL: Harold Shaw Pub., 1989.

Rainer, Thom S. and Eric Geiger. *Simple Church: Returning to God's Process for Making Disciples.* Nashville: B&H Publishing Group, 2011.

Ray, Bruce A. *Celebrating the Sabbath: Finding Rest in a Restless World.* Phillipsburg, NJ: P&R Pub., 2000.

Reich, Frank. "Competition and Creation." *IIIM Magazine Online*, v. 4, no. 6 (Feb. 11- 17, 2002), pp. 1-9. http://thirdmill.org/magazine/issues.asp/volume/4/number/6 Accessed 8 Apr. 2013.

Roques, Mark and Jim Ticknor. *Fields of God: Football and the Kingdom of God.* Carlisle, PA: Authentic Lifestyles, 2003.

Sauer, Erich. *In the Arena of Faith: A Call to a Consecrated Life.* Grand Rapids, MI: Eerdmans, 1955.

Sjogren, Steven, Dave Ping, Doug Pollock. *Irresistible Evangelism*. Loveland, CO: Group, 2004.

Smith, Jimmy and English, Greg, eds. *Sports Ministry That Wins: How to Initiate, Build, and Manage a Sports Ministry Program*. Canton, OH: Overwhelming Victory Press. 2017.

Spalding, Greg. *Run the Greatest Race: Be a Disciple Who Makes a Difference*. Pittsburgh, PA: City of Champions Pub. Co., 1996.

Sport: An Educational and Pastoral Challenge: Seminar of Study on the Theme of Sport Chaplains, Vatican, 7-8 September 2007 / Catholic Church. Pontificium Consilium pro Laicis. Citta del Vaticano: Libreria Editrice Vaticana, 2008.

Sports Ambassadors (Website): www.onechallenge.org/go/sports-ambassadors/

Stanley, Andy. *Louder than Words*. Sisters, OR: Multnomah Press, 2004.

Stoll, Sharon Kay and Jennifer M. Beller. *Who Says This is Cheating? : Anybody's Sports Ethics Book*. Dubuque, IA: Kendall Hunt Publishing, 1993.

Strobel, Lee. *Inside the Mind of Unchurched Harry and Mary: How to Reach Friends and Family Who Avoid God and the Church*. Grand Rapids, MI: Zondervan , 1993.

Takamizama, Eiko. "Religious Commitment Theory: A Model of Japanese Christians." *Torch Trinity Journal*.

Thiessen, Gordon. *Cross Training Manual: Playbook for Christian Athletes*. Grand Island, NE: Cross Training Pub., 1991.

Tinley, Josh. *Kneeling in the End Zone: Spiritual Lessons from the World of Sports*. Cleveland, OH: Pilgrim Press, 2009.

Verhey, Allen. *The Great Reversal: Ethics and the New Testament*. Grand Rapids, MI: Eerdmans, 1984.

Walker, Dan. *Sport and Sundays : Christian TV Presenter Dan Walker Tells His Story.* Rev. and Updated Ed. Leominster, Eng.: Day One Publications, 2010, c2009.

Warner, Gary. *Competition.* Elgin, IL: David Cook, 1979.

Webb, Bernice Larson. *The Basketball Man: James Naismith.* Lawrence: University Press of Kansas, 1973.

Wier, Stuart. *Kriss.* London: Marshall Pickering, 1996.

_____. *More Than Champions: A Sport Stars' Secrets of Success.* London: Harper Collins, 1993.

_____. *The Ultimate Prize: Great Christian Olympians.* London: Hodder Christian, 2004.

_____. *What the Book Says About Sport.* Oxford, Eng.: Bible Reading Fellowship, 2000.

Young, David C. *A Brief History of the Olympic Games.* Malden, MA: Blackwell Pub., 2004.

Major Sponsors

First Friends Church

- Offering comprehensive Sports, Recreation and Fitness opportunities for all ages
- Contact Information:
  5455 Market Ave., Canton, OH 44714
- www.firstfriends.org

Logan Family Foundation

- Logan Sports Inc. offers a comprehensive line of Sportswear and Sporting Goods giving special discounts to CSRM Associate Partners
- Contact Information:
  Logan Sports, 1144 S. Main Street,
  North Canton, OH 44720
- www.LoganFamilyFoundation.org

CPSIA information can be obtained
at www.ICGtesting.com
Printed in the USA
FSHW021951020721
82938FS